THE NUDGE

Life Is Calling, Wake Up

By Felicia Shaviri

As You Wish Publishing, LLC

Kyra@asyouwishpublishing.com 602-592-1141

ISBN-13: 978-1-7324982-7-3

ISBN-10: 1-7324982-7-X

Edited by Todd Schaefer

Printed in the United States of America.

Dedication

To my parents Cleveland and Ola V. Pryor, my heart overflows with joy knowing that I chose you. To my beautiful mother-n-law Nargis Shaviri my heart will always remember the warmth of your laughter and your unconditional love for all. My husband, and my beautiful children Jasmine, Micah and Cyrus, my hope is that you tap into your inner strengths and always live fearlessly.

Table of Contents

Foreword by Chauncey Beaty

I was visiting a friend in Seattle for a week. One afternoon, she had to work, and I had the entire day to myself. I looked on Eventbrite to see what was going on locally and ran across a speaker's training. I arrived with great excitement, found a seat in a middle row, and opened my heart to listen. To my surprise, the event was hosted by a former employee of Trump (who was still very much aligned with his politics) and this very blue, highly diverse city of Seattle was not having it.

During the break, a crowd of women were gathered in the bathroom in protest. They were mad and vocal. It was fascinating. I'm from South Carolina where politics play out differently. As I listened and occasionally tried to bring in my voice, I locked eyes with Felicia—the golden woman, whose short curly hair and hazel skin were nearly identical in color. I knew her upset was not merely about the politics. Similar to me, she was hoping to get *something* profound and life-changing from the event. We started to talk. "I'm sure there is something to learn here," I said. "At minimum, look at his marketing strategy. Look how many people he was able to get in this bathroom," I said in jest. I could see Felicia starting to calm down. We chatted some more, and she shared with me that she had just quit her job in law enforcement and that she was starting to follow her gut and the divine "nudges" she was getting. She was in search of *something* more. I invited her to my annual Ready Woman Retreat that was coming up in the next week. One week later, Felicia joined us in a circle of women who were ready to heal and fearlessly come alive. That was three years ago.

I've watched Felicia in tears when she trusted the "nudge" even though it didn't make sense to her and others. Sometimes the outcome was the loss of a friend or a breakdown in the relationship. I've also witnessed that same decision that appeared to rattle her world open unimaginable doors and offer Felicia access to the highest levels of joy and feelings of accomplishment that she's ever experienced.

So often when our soul is yearning for more and we are looking for that *something* to fulfill us, we go on a journey of acquisition: consuming, looking outside ourselves, and not listening to that voice deep inside that says, "go there," "speak to him," or "do this." Scripture tells us that God has plans for us that will prosper us and not harm us, but here is a hard truth: most of us will not get to experience the highest plans of God. We simply do not trust enough, are not connected enough to hear God, and certainly not obedient enough to take action. Felicia is a great teacher for us on what's possible when you trust divine inspiration and forge on a journey of self-expression. This book provides us with tangible, practical ways to let go and let God.

Introduction

Nudge: to touch or push gently; to prod lightly, urge into action.

You know that feeling that you sometimes get, but you can't quite put your finger on it? Like that time, you were waiting to catch the train, but decided for no apparent reason to stop at the drugstore? And once you got there, you forgot why you went in the first place? As a result, you missed boarding the normal commuter train home and had to wait for the next one.

As you await the arrival of the train, a thought about a former college friend enters your mind again. This particular friend has been on and off your mind for several weeks. You wonder how life is for them if they were doing well. Just last week, you crossed paths with a mutual friend you knew but hadn't seen or heard from in some time. The two of you chat for a bit, wish one another well, and continue on.

As the train approaches, you stand, the doors open, and you step onto the train. You begin to search for the nearest seat but stop when you hear someone call your name. The sound of the voice is familiar to you, but maybe a voice you've not heard in a long time. They call out your name again, and instantaneously there is a smile that appears on your face so wide that it pushes your ears into your hairline. Overwhelmed with joy, you're freaking out inside as you start the conversation with them by saying, "I was *just* thinking about you! What a coincidence!" But really, was it?

You find out they're doing great. Shortly after graduation, they landed a great job for one of the accounting firms in Tucson, Arizona. Later that same year, they got married and now have a set of twins, Melia and Malachi. Time flies, especially when you hear that she and her husband just celebrated their tenth wedding anniversary. As the conversation comes to a close, you exchange phone numbers and see that your stop is arriving. You both say your goodbyes, and you find yourself standing on the platform long after the train has departed, in awe of what just happened.

Have you thought about a subject you've wanted to know more about and shortly after found a book or magazine that helped you understand yourself better. Maybe you found your new treasure at a garage sale or in a collection that a friend was going to donate, and it was exactly what you were seeking without realizing you were looking for it? It showed up for you out of the blue?

Maybe there was a thought about getting into film or acting, and you take notice of an ad for a casting call in your local coffee shop. You audition and don't get the role, but while waiting to audition, you meet someone who would grow to be significant in your life? So maybe it wasn't about the audition, but the creation of a relationship. Would you look at any of these scenarios as a coincidence and just blow it off, or have you ever wondered if there was more to it and decided to follow the feeling?

Introduction

Do you think this book you're holding is happenstance or coincidence? When was the last time you had a coincidence? Do you think of them as common occurrences? Have you ever had more than one during your waking hours? Or are you just completely lost by what I am saying, but are curious to understand?

I don't believe in luck, coincidence or happenstance. What I've come to realize is that life has a way of sending us clues through the ways of that distinct feeling that we get from time to time, and it is only when we decide to go with the flow of that unseen force or energy source that will lead us to live a life beyond what we could've ever imagined.

March 2014

What appeared to have been a mere coincidence on a bone-chilling spring day in downtown Chicago would cause the life I once knew to shatter into tiny pieces over nearly three years. I would find myself on a journey that would lead me to uncover a realization of being connected to everyone and everything. From my first breath of the day and the rising sun, everyone that would cross my path, regardless of their status or the interaction, I would find the beauty in it. I felt a connection to the trees, hopping bunnies, frightened coyote and the beautiful stream of water as it flowed out of the drain pipe on a trail.

I was in awe with all of it! It was as if I was seeing life for the first time. The sun was breathtaking, and I could hardly wait to show my gratitude upon rising by being in its amazing presence as it greeted the world.

The most fascinating discovery would be the moment I began to realize the strength, courage, and wisdom within that would lead me to love all unconditionally. I would never have imagined how much my life would go from who I thought I was, due to a series of “coincidences” in a blink of an eye. I had been in the driver’s seat all along. I was living a life that I had created, even if it was by default. So, without further ado, won’t you lend me your ear? I would love to tell you a story.

Spirituality: Is God Real?

If you tried to talk to me about spirituality, I would've shut it down. I wasn't hearing it any of it. One thing is for sure, I would never have imagined how much my life would change from who I thought I was, to who I am now. All due to a series of "coincidences," which happened in the blink of an eye.

Look, I'm a black female from the south side of Chicago (Englewood, as a matter of fact) where you can find some of the best barbeque, hole-in-the-wall live entertainment and gospel churches attached to liquor stores on every other block. Growing up, my sibling and I were never pressured to attend Sunday church services, like some of the other kids we knew from school or the neighborhood. My mother believed in free will and the importance of choosing your own path when it came to religion or spirituality.

She believed that was personal for the individual and it should be on their terms and pace; otherwise, it would be more of being brainwashed. Now if you had questions surrounding God and religion, she was always open to it for discussion and shared with you what she knew or had been told. My mother could answer our questions in a way that would fascinate me because she would leave you to think about the answer. I remember growing up and periodically going to my grandmother's church on 89th and Ashland. My goodness, what a gala that was! You might have thought it was Easter Sunday with the way everyone was all dressed up. My thoughts were that everybody was good in the eyes of God, as a child, even if they did something wrong, but that belief wouldn't last long.

As I grew older, my brain would ache from the confusion of the church from seeing all the hypocrisy and contradictions following the Sunday sermon. As a child, and even today as an adult, I could not understand why what you wore to church had so much to do with attending the services. At some of the other churches, I didn't understand why people placed money in the donation boxes, knelt in front of the statues, or lit candles and prayed before them.

Every time I tried to ask someone a question about anything having to do with the church or religion, I was told it was a sin to question God, and if I kept it up, I was going to burn in hell forever. I believed them, especially after having overheard a conversation between two of my older brothers when I was about five or six years old. I'll never forget it. I was sitting on a stump near a dirt patch that never managed to grow grass due to the foot traffic and my mud pie creations.

Mitch: "You know someday this is all going to end."

Dennis: "What's going to end?"

Mitch: "This, the whole wide world is going to end."

(I couldn't help but be confused at that point, and I wanted him to tell Dennis what he was talking about.)

Dennis: "How? What do you mean? The world is not going to end."

Mitch: "Yes, it is. It says so in the Bible. Like the first time it ended, it ended in water, and the next time it's supposed to be with fire. Everything is going to burn; the whole world is going to be on fire."

Dennis: "For real?"

Mitch: "Yeah, and everything is going to get burnt up, even the hor-sees."

My heart dropped into my shoes. I suddenly had a lump in my throat, and I wanted to release the scream that was building within my little body, but I couldn't. I knew if I did, my brothers were going to get upset with me for eavesdropping on their conversation and it may have made matters worse. They didn't even know I was there. My body was frozen and filled with fear. I couldn't move. But the horses; I began to imagine people running down the street in flames screaming, the trees next to our house on fire, our house on fire. My imagination was endless, and I wondered where we would go for safety. Would there be anywhere we could go? Not having a safe place for kids and good people to go when the world was on fire seemed like a pretty mean thing to do, especially if God loves us all. Besides, it must be true because one of my big brothers said it, and he knew about a lot of stuff, well, more than I did at that time anyway.

I never mentioned a word of what I heard to a single soul. Instead, I made a deal with God. After countless nights of not sleeping and being completely stressed about dying with the horses, I pleaded with him not to let me die and explained to him that I wasn't ready as I reminded him that I was just a little kid. Now the question to myself was, "How would God know when I was ready to die?" That was when I decided to create a special hand clap that only he and I knew that would let him know I was ready. The deal was no matter how upset he may be with the world he wouldn't end it unless I did the special hand clap. You want to talk superhero powers? Pamela Grier, also known as Foxy Brown, didn't have anything on me. Hell, I was responsible for saving the world from being burnt up, and I was still in kindergarten. But I do have a confession. For the longest time after making that deal with God, I would not clap my hands for anyone or anything, not because I didn't want to, but because I forgot the clap sequence. My thinking was if I clap my hands, it could be a beginning to the end. Well, I forgot the sequence. Oh, my goodness, the thoughts that run through the minds of little kids. It makes me want to carry a pocket full of shiny pennies and give them one for sharing their thoughts.

When I was about fourteen years old, I realized that I didn't want to live in fear anymore of the world coming to an end. I didn't want to be afraid of all the stories I had been told by others when it came to pleasing God. Being kind to myself and others was the road I decided to take. I thought God would be pleased with that, and if not, I was shooting for purgatory. After all, it was better than hell, right? It would give him time to think about some of the good things I did and could give me a chance to still get into heaven.

I could say the world opened to me, or maybe I should say I opened my heart to the world and my life would never be the same. I began to have a series of coincidences, one after another. There were days when I lost count of the amount of "coincidences."

My interest in going to church became less and less, and the only reason I would go was to hang out with my Grandma Flynn. Then I would find myself getting in trouble for talking in church and eventually found myself going less until I stopped going. After all, it wasn't that important to me anyway.

My grandmother was the coolest, most hip ever granny I knew, and everyone loved her at least from what I could see. She had a "side hustle" going on long before the term became popular: babysitting a handful of kids while their parents went to work for a fraction of the cost of taking them to a daycare. Most of the families lived in the apartment building my grandmother lived in; the rest didn't have to travel far to get to her. We were all fairly close in age and played together during my family visits to her place.

Grandma Flynn had a way of making you feel special and loved without having to mutter a word. She could look into your eyes, and you felt like the most precious gift ever. Don't get me wrong; she wasn't a softie either. She loved most sports, soap operas, believed in God and seemed to enjoy the warmth of our smiles as we devoured slices of her homemade pound cake. If you spent the night at her place, you were going to get on those knees before bed and recite the "Now I Lay Me Down to Sleep" prayer along with a two in the morning wake up call for a "potty check," so there were no chances of you wetting the bed.

After my Grandma Flynn's death was my sister Gwen's, and I think I began to look at life and death with less of an emotional attachment and an understanding of it being their time. After my mom passed, I ended up with my Grandma's Bible, and although I didn't read it consistently, there have been times that I've picked it up and put it down. Sometimes we aren't ready to receive what we aren't ready for but having it near me as a reminder that although she's no longer here in the physical, she will always be a part of my experience. What I began to realize was that I didn't have to follow anyone's rules to have a connection to anything, and the same goes for you. Just do your best to live your life in a kind and caring way, and usually, it turns out alright. God, the Universe, Source, whoever knows us better than anyone else ever will.

The Shift

What was happening to me? Could I be having a midlife crisis? Is this what menopause felt like? Was it that "Change of Life" thingy that old people talk about? What the hell? Maybe I was on the verge of a nervous breakdown, or my mental health wellness needed an evaluation. What if it was in the early stages? Fuck! Why? No, no, no. This cannot be happening to me. Okay, but it is. Something is happening here, and I don't know who I can talk to about it. The thought of me losing my mind or sharing what I was experiencing with someone who may not understand terrified me, so I kept it to myself for a while.

It was something beyond explainable through words. I wanted to run away from it like I'd done so many times in the past. It seemed every time I attempted to leave this "weird sense of knowing" behind, it always found a way back to me. Over the years, I had come to shove that "feeling" I was having so deep inside that I had forgotten it existed. Sure, I managed to escape it over the years by staying busy and creating continuous goals that would make me feel like I was being super productive for months or even years at a time, but it continued to come back.

This time, it was different. This time, it was clearer than the previous. This time, I knew I was being summoned by a presence that I could not see or hear, but I could feel, and it was so gentle and calming. I was ready and willing to trust like never before that I was here to do something far greater than I could have imagined. I struggled to explain what I was feeling and seldom shared my experience with my husband or children for fear of being judged or having someone suggest I see a professional, again.

There were many nights when I would cry silently as I slept on the living room sofa with my best friend and soulmate who chose me during a visit to the Tacoma Humane Society, Jaeger. He seemed to understand me perfectly well. He loved me just as I was. He loved me unconditionally, and others may have seen him as simply being an animal, a dog, but I knew different.

I was looking at the world through a completely different set of lenses. Someone or something had cleaned and sanitized my view with super-duper Windex. I'm not kidding. Although everything appeared to be so clear and simple from my point of view, my loved ones desperately struggled to understand and make sense of what was happening to their wife and mother.

The world in which they had known and were familiar with was becoming more challenging to understand for everyone, including me. The only difference was I wasn't afraid of the unknown.

One thing was for sure, I could not go back to being who I once thought myself to be. Every time I tried, it would cause such turmoil. The only option was to go forward regardless of the outcome. Sound pretty intense? Trust me when I say you have no idea.

I decided to return to Chicago for the services of one of my best friends from high school. Each time I would visit, I typically stayed with my sister Deb on the south side of the city. But this time, instead of staying with my sister, I opted to stay at a hotel in downtown Chicago with another high school friend who had flown up from Arizona for the services as well.

I don't remember the exact date, but I do remember it was the day I let go and allowed myself to create a keen sense of awareness, to everything and everyone. The funeral services were to take place the following day, and neither of us rented a car, so Carolyn and I decided to hang out at the hotel. I was training for a figure/bodybuilding competition, so I didn't want to be tempted to eat anything that would cause me to go off my training plan. It was late afternoon, leading into the evening when we decided to go out for a bite to eat.

Throughout high school, we were both talkers when we were in the company of one another. If you were sharing the same floor, you were sure to hear two "chatty Kathys" meandering down the hall laughing and giggling nonstop. We pressed the elevator to go down to the lobby. When it reached our floor, we entered the car, taking notice that there was a gentleman dressed in a wool trench with a gray and black scarf around his neck. He was clean-shaven and quite handsome, late twenties or early thirties perhaps. I became a bit reserved, but Carolyn was still laughing about something we were discussing.

Carolyn: (She looks at him) "Hello? You sho' smell good."

Felicia: (Sighs and mutters) “Carolyn?”

Carolyn: (Turns to face me) “What? He do!”

Carolyn: (Looks at the young man) “You just getting off work? Do you work here?”

GM: “No, um…No I don’t.”

Carolyn: “Oh…What do you do?”

GM: “I’m a…uh…I’m a personal trainer.”

Carolyn: “Ha…that’s so funny, that what she is…she’s a personal trainer too. What a coincidence!”

We exited the hotel lobby and stood in the middle of the sidewalk trying to decide which direction we should go in search of food. A different gentleman was walking by us when I said, “Excuse me, could you recommend a place for us to grab a bite to eat?” He then responded with, “I’m sorry I can’t. I’m from Seattle and I’m just visiting. Sorry.” Carolyn began to laugh and said, “Really? That’s where she’s from too!”

Internally, I had already begun to wonder what the chances were of having two commonalities with complete strangers while visiting my home town. As quickly as I attempted to shake it off, Carolyn turned in my direction looking me dead in the eyes and said, “Felicia, another coincidence? Girl, I think somebody is trying to talk to you!”

I looked at Carolyn straight-faced to let her know I didn’t find any humor in what had just happened.

I immediately told Carolyn to shut her face and to keep that “God stuff” over on her side of the street. I wasn’t in the mood to hear any of that spiritual stuff about anything that was happening. She continued to look at me and laugh.

As simple as these little "coincidences" may have appeared to most people, it was just the start of what was to come. As we continued to walk down in search of food, I experienced two additional "coincidences," making a total of four of those in less than a two-hour window. I could not at that moment, remember anything remotely similar to what I was experiencing.

We finally stumbled upon a sports pub with decent grub and had a few more laughs as we were returning to our hotel. I was grateful to not have any additional "coincidences" before going to bed. Although, I must admit I was a bit curious about the chances of someone having four coincidental encounters, and as I began to close my eyes, I wondered if there would be more.

More than Chance

Morning came quickly, and although I'm an early riser, I felt a bit cheated out of my sleep. Perhaps it was the encounters of yesterday evening that roamed through my mind as I slept. As I looked from the hotel window out on the city, I thought to myself, "She's really gone." I didn't feel sad, but a bit numb and sometimes angry about all of the crap she was dealing with in her final days, but it was what is.

I had become a member of the (National Physique Committee) NPC Figure/Bodybuilding competitor in 2012 and was currently in training for an upcoming show in April which was less than six weeks out. My cardio routine was pretty intense, and it was important that I not miss a session for any reason, so I got dressed, threw on my workout gear and headed to the hotel gym.

I took a peek through the window and wanted to jump and scream because there was not a soul there. I went in, checking out the equipment, treadmills, elliptical and free-weights. I put my headphones on with one of my favorite tunes playing, and I decide to work arms. I was on my second set when a woman walked through the door of the gym. She said good morning, and I replied and continued lifting. I could feel someone was watching me and I turned to see she was in the same spot the entire time. My thoughts were, "Uh, what the hell are you looking at? Why are you standing there staring at me? Surely you're old enough to have been taught that it's rude to stare." Then something happened. I placed the dumbbell that was in my left hand on the bench, removed one of my earbuds and asked her a question.

Felicia: "Are you okay?"

Pam: "Who me? Oh yeah, I'm okay."

Felicia: "Are you sure? I mean…"

Pam: "Oh yeah, I 'm fine." (Pause…awkward silence)

Felicia: "Okay." (Picks up the weight again)

Pam: (In a shaky voice as she nodded her head and looked around the room) "Umm…You know what?…Can I tell you something? Umm…umm…I'm not okay. I'm really not okay, I could really use a hug right now."

Without hesitation, I placed the dumbbell on the bench and took a couple of steps away from it as I replied, "Well come on over here and get one," with my arms wide open—and she did. What the heck was I doing? This woman was a complete stranger, and I was offering to give her a hug? This was not something you would ever find me doing, but maybe with my kids or husband. Hell, I didn't really do this with my siblings. Are you kidding me?

She began to cry as we hugged, followed by an apology for staring at me as I was working out and now interrupting me for a hug. I told her not to worry about it and thanked her for giving me a reason to take a longer than normal break, and I told her that it would be okay.

Pam was in her late forties, married to a college professor and mother of one son who was nine. She expressed how extremely exhausted she was with everything and felt as though she was being pulled in so many directions; she could hardly keep up.

She went on to explain her son was so young because she and her husband wanted to get their careers on track, see the world and have fun before settling down to start a family. Now she found it quite challenging to keep up with a nine-year-old that doesn't know how to be still. She was also helping care for her husband's mother who was elderly and needed constant assistance. Because the husband didn't want anyone outside of the home like a CNA to care for his mother, Pam was expected to step up and help.

We laughed together as we talked about all of the expectations of being a wife and a mother. We wanted to find the idiot woman who gave society the false truth about women being phenomenal super-beings. Maybe it was that stupid ad years ago: "I can bring home the bacon, fry it up in the pan and never let you forget…blah, blah, blah."

In any case, I suggested that she try not to be so hard on herself. I reminded her that we could only do our best at any given moment and told her not to forget about making time for herself. She thanked me for the hug as she wiped the remaining tears, then she said:

Pam: "I have to say you look amazing, by the way."

Felicia: "Oh, thanks!"

Pam: "Have you always been in such great shape? You must've played sports in high school or something because your body is like, wow. I could probably stand to be in the gym more often. But I just want to say you look great! If you don't mind my asking, what do you do for work?"

Felicia: "Well, I'm a Corrections Deputy for one of the sheriff's departments out of Washington State. I'm also a personal trainer, and I do voice-over work. I was the voice at the Seattle Budget Rent-A-Car Call Center for nearly fifteen years. I was also not aware that people could make a living off of their voice, but that's another story."

When I shared with Pam that I did voice-over work, she lit up and said, "I knew it! I could hear it in your voice. Have you had anyone tell you that your voice is soothing? I mean really, you have a lovely tone." She continued, "I would like to give you my information. I create e-learning software by the way, and I think your voice would be perfect for some of the programs, if you're interested.

I accepted the offer to stay in contact and noticed how limited my time was now that I'd not completed even half of my normal routine. So, I wished her well and let her know I needed to complete my workout. She nodded, apologized and told me that she'd be right back. When she returned, I was on the treadmill as she handed me a Post-it note with her contact information on it.

Sometime after returning home to Washington State, I found the Post-it note Pam had written her information on in my cross-body bag and decided to give her a call. After the call ended, I decided I would put her information in my cell phone and throw away the tattered note. A couple of weeks or so later, I found myself in a hurry running home from the gym and needed to get out of the house for work quickly. I started a load of laundry and washed the cell phone! And that "rice trick" is a myth—total bologna—so you already know all information was lost.

Pam and I never spoke again following that call, but nearly two years later, would you believe I officially became a voiceover talent? You got it, I found myself in the home studio of a former coworker recording audiobooks that can be found on Amazon. It's pretty amazing at how that works. All you have to do is think, feel, believe and be it, and it will undoubtedly come to fruition. It may not happen right away, but it will when you are ready for it.

Time For Church

The day came for us to head over to the church for my dear friend's send off. I was feeling overwhelmed with emotions. I wanted to laugh, cry, and even seek out those who failed to be there for her in her final days, but what would that solve? It didn't matter anymore. As we came nearer to the church, I began to have conversations in my head about whether I should call out those that were near her in her last days who caused her heartache and her condition to worsen. She needed them to be there for her and not judge her about her decision to file for a divorce! She was gone.

As we walked into Jackson Fellowship Church, it was a packed house with standing room only. There were many of our former classmates in attendance to pay their last respects. I took a seat in one of the back pews between my sister Deb and my dear friend, Carolyn.

You could hear her mom sobbing, and I looked up to see her son Eric who still had the baby face I remembered. It's amazing how quickly time passes when you don't take the time to slow down. This sounds like something my mother and her friends would say: "It seemed like just yesterday I was changing your diaper." The organ began playing that tune that always makes you want to cry and be sad, which is something I never quite understood about funerals. As a lump began rising in my throat, I found myself glancing around the church at those who came to bid my friend farewell, wanting to make sure no one was watching me to see if I was crying. As much as I tried to ward it off, my eyes filled with tears and my stomach became knotted as my mind again reminded me—she's gone. I looked at my sister and Carolyn and thanked them for coming with me and being there for me. I could hear words being said to me, "Breathe Felicia. Just breathe. She's all good now, no more chemo or pain. Be happy for her." In that instant, I agreed and let go.

So, as I sat there trying to find a reason to be happy for my now deceased friend, all I was hearing from the preacher as he stood at the podium delivering his sermon was 'Blah, blah, blah, blah, blah.' I know, awful right? But if God knows everything like they say he does, well, he already knew what I was thinking before I shared it. As I said earlier, going to church wasn't my thing, and I wasn't feeling any different being there for her services.

Preacher number two stepped up to the podium and got my attention right away. I quieted my mind just a tad and looked at him and thought to myself, "That man is show-nuff fine as hell." I found myself thinking out loud without realizing it and Carolyn told me to be quiet and stop sinning. I chuckled as I rolled my eyes thinking, "Whatever."

Seriously though, have you ever had a thought like that and you knew it was wrong, but you didn't give a crap? I felt drawn to him, and I would say it was definitely not proper because I couldn't tell you anything he had said. It was all 'Blah, blah blah' too. I couldn't help but whisper to Carolyn, "Now you don't think him fine? I bet he smell good too." Again I was scolded and told I was going to burn in hell if I kept it up. Reluctantly, I digressed. After all, I was in the house of the Lord. "I'll be quiet, but I don't have to stop looking," I whispered to her.

I tried to get him off my mind and even wondered if he was wearing that Stetson cologne from the commercial that used to be on television. I thought how delightful it would be to meet him, say hello and get close enough to smell his cologne. I was cracking myself up with my sinful thoughts. Not that I was thinking about having an affair with the man or anything, but if you followed all the rules from the good book, I was a total sinner just with my thinking.

Once again, the organ began to play concluding the services which took longer than I had imagined it would, but thank goodness we were finally out of there. The mourners began to stand and slowly left their pews, moving towards the altar to give their final condolences to the family and view the body one last time.

As we began to exit the church, the cold wind whipped around us as if it were angry, causing people to make a mad dash to their vehicles, but not before smiling for a group photo with high school peers that were in attendance. Patricia would've been pleased to have seen how many of our former classmates showed up to her service to pay their respects. I decided to opt out of attending the repass at her mothers home, I wasn't in the mood to pretend that all was well when it wasn't.

Anytime I returned home, I always made it a point to stop by some of my favorite hometown eateries. Today, I was up for an Italian beef sandwich. My sister suggested Portillo's restaurant, which was about five miles from the church. We arrived at the restaurant, found a booth near a window, and walked up to place our order. We were given a numbered ticket that would be called when our order was ready. I still found myself thinking about that preacher, only now, I was trying to figure out why was I so drawn to him and I couldn't stop smiling.

Just as we were completing our lunch, I began to feel the flutter of butterflies, same as I did in the church. I thought to myself, "What the hell is my problem?" At that very moment, three pastors entered the restaurant. They were the same pastors that spoke at my friend's funeral. Maybe it was me, but I could instantly feel my smile widen at the sight of him. He was quite handsome, standing about 6'2," thin in stature, but he was wearing the heck out of that clergy collar. So why not request a photo with the three? That's exactly what I did. He made it a point to stand in close to me, and that was how I was able to take in his scent, and it was truly breathtaking, Oh and I think it was Halston.

I know my behavior was not virtuous, but it felt good to have him place his hand on the small of my back and then completely around my waist, pulling me in close to him as the photo was taken. I told him it was nice to meet him, requested that he pray for me and wished him well. What? Did you miss the part where I asked him to pray for me?

Long after we had left, I found myself sitting at the airport awaiting my return back to Seattle, thinking about all of the events, experiences and coincidences during my visit to Chicago. I met Pam: the lady who created e-learning programs. I had thoughts of meeting the sexy and handsome preacher at my friend's funeral. I couldn't help but be in awe. What if there was a meaning behind it all, and what if there was someone or something beyond what I could understand trying to communicate with me? Better still, what if some or all of what was happening to me was happening to other people, but they were like me and weren't making the connection to them either? Then I wondered if my eldest sister was right. Maybe I was reading too much into what was happening. After all, she had warned me earlier in the year about how delicate the mind was and suggested I be careful not to go overboard; otherwise, I could find myself on the other side of craziness.

What I had come to realize on my flight home was a feeling that there was more to what I had experienced. Although I didn't know what to make of it all, there was an undeniable knowing within—there was more to come, and it would take my willingness to be open and receptive towards the world around me like never before.

Punched In The Gut

I remember it like it was yesterday. I was off, and my husband had cooked one of his delicious dishes: beef biryani. One of my best friends, Janice, was quite a fan of this dish so I decided to pack some in one of my Rubbermaid containers (that I wouldn't get back for a hundred years) and take her some for lunch.

Being a morning person has always been a gift to me compared to most people I know. Sleeping in past 6 am has always been a challenge for me. The morning has always been a magical time of the day for as far back as I can remember. There was beauty in the silence and stillness. Sometimes you could even take your imagination on a wild ride wherever you wanted to go, just to escape it all.

There wasn't any traffic because it was a weekend day, so I parked in front of the jail near the entrance, closer to the gym and locker rooms. I was feeling great! I was excited and looking forward to surprising my best friend with lunch. I entered the locker room dancing and singing, not much different than any other time, but what happened next will forever be deeply seated in my brain.

Me: “Hey Janis Vicente’!! What up girl? How yo momma is? I brought you some good eats. The man that I’m married to made a ton of biryani.”

Janice (With a warm smile) “Yes, umm, good, cause I didn’t bring my lunch today.”

Me: “What’s going on Jay-Vee?”

Janice: “Nada.”

Me: “Oh okay. You ain’t got a 411 for me?”

Janice: “Nope, not that I can think of.”

Me: “I feel good Janice Vicente’! I feel like dancing. I want to go shake my groove thang! Hahaha! (laughter) I could really use a drink and some loud music. You wanna go dancing with me, Janice Vicente’?”

Janice: “Umm, hahaha, not really Dookie.” (It’s a long story, but yes that’s her pet name for me and, no I didn’t poop on myself).

Me: “Well okay, I guess I’ll holla at you later then. I’ma head back to the house where my fam-ma-lee be.”

Janice: “Oh wait. Speaking of going out, we were trying to coordinate our days because we were thinking about doing an intervention.”

Me: “What? An intervention?”

Me: (Excitedly laughing, steps into Janice and whispers) “Oh, so you do got some 411?”

Janice: (Giggles as she looks at me)

Me: “Doing an intervention...and who is ‘we’?”

Janice: “Me, Ramsey and Jatsky.”

Me: “Who are y’all doing an intervention on? Who, Janice Vicente’? Come on, Janice Vicente’, tell me, please, please, please tell me!”

Janice: “We are thinking about doing an intervention on you, Dook.”

As she looked into my eyes, I asked, “An intervention on me, Janice Vicente? On me?” For the first time in a very long time, someone was able to see straight through me. I felt like my equilibrium was off and I was lightheaded and dizzy at the same time. Once I processed what she had actually said to me, it felt like a linebacker dressed in full gear had run full on and rammed into my stomach, and I flew against the wall of the locker room and slowly crumbled to the floor cradling my head in my hands and began to sob.

Don’t ask me what happened next because I couldn’t tell you if I wanted to. I don’t even remember how I got home. It was as if everything from that moment on went blank. My entire world as I knew it would never be the same. It shook my entire existence to the core, and I could feel it. It’s like when you have a ding from a stone in your windshield, you can still drive the car provided you don’t continue to have more stones causing damage. But if you do, it is inevitable they will cause the windshield to crack and spread to the point where you have no other choice but to replace it. Only thing is, the experience hadn’t completely processed, and it would take some time. It was at that very moment that I would realize what true friendship was. My windshield was definitely cracked, and it was spreading faster than I could keep up with it.

Janice and I would not revisit what happened that day in the locker room for several months. The next time that I would speak about it would be as a guest speaker for a women's business networking group. Two of my best friends would come to show their support, but only one of them would be reminded of the event. Even then, she was not aware of the impact it had on my life. There wasn't a dry eye in the studio as I concluded my experience. Many of the women spoke to me after and shared how powerful and inspiring my journey was to them and how they saw themselves in my story. I was giving out hugs and kisses with ease, and I encouraged them to believe in themselves as much as I believed in them and to trust they would find their way.

I too found myself being inspired that night as I drove home after that meeting. Instead of stepping out of the box, I had jumped out of the box. It was incredible to know that by sharing my story, I was able to help others see their own and that made me really happy. It made me feel good about my path in life, and I knew it was only the beginning.

You Ask For It

Cleaning House
September 2015

It started off as a normal day. I got up in the morning, did my cardio, showered in the locker room and headed upstairs to the jail. I was the Clinic Escort Officer, and for the most part, it was a pretty good gig. My main duty was to maintain safety and security for all those coming or going in and out of the medical area of the county jail. It was a fairly laid-back position, but there was always that underlying possibility of having a jack in the box that could send your day into a tailspin in a matter of seconds.

Keep in mind, the clinic could be one of the most dangerous places other than the kitchen due to the access of utensils and tools that if concealed by an inmate and returned to a housing unit could cause some major issues for all and result in someone being hurt badly, if not killed. There was a lot that was happening within the facility, a lot of unrest not only for the inmates, but for everyone.

Don't get me wrong, I am very humble for having had the opportunity to work with such an incredibly talented and gifted group of human beings, both officers and inmates alike. I learned a ton from working within the confinements of the jail to include paying attention to how it was beginning to affect me. I noticed officers who had only been working at the jail less than a year changing, becoming hard and desensitized because it was an unspoken requirement to remember it was "us vs. them" at the end of the day. Some officers would dread coming into work before they got there. Many often had a tremendous amount of responsibility: kids in college, new homes, cars, paying for a wedding, and family vacations. Even the toughest officer had a big heart at the jail, although they wouldn't let others see it, and that goes for me too.

There was clearly a change that was taking place with me, and I didn't know who I could talk to about it, so I just kept it inside. I struggled not to share my private life with anyone other than Janice or Dayna, were both like sisters to me, besides, sharing my private life wasn't the way I rolled. During some of the downtime in the clinic, I wondered why the feeling that I was missing something was occurring and lingering more often than before.

I would open the file cabinet and begin to organize it, throwing out old notes, files, and rosters that were no longer of use. Over the next few weeks, I had cleared out most of the items in my work area. It wouldn't be until years later that I would realize I had been preparing to leave the family I'd known for years.

Thinking back now, it was as if something was moving through me and preparing me for the next phase of my journey.

Esther Who?

I had been looking for a solution, a clue, or anything that would help give me some direction on which way to go for years whenever that feeling would come. One thing I knew for certain was that each time I would ignore that feeling the next time it would return it was stronger than the last.

Then I noticed it. It was a book and the title was *Ask and It Is Given* by Esther Hicks/Abraham. I didn't quite know what to make of the book. It was lying on the bottom shelf of my desk, and it appeared to be one that was donated to the jail by someone, and I knew that because it was marked with the initials of the jail. I thought about taking the dang thing, but that voice was in my head: "Are you seriously going to take that? Now you know that would be stealing. Besides, you make enough money; go buy the damn thing if you want it that bad."

As the days passed, I continued to notice the book. Sometimes I would just look at it, then look away, then look at it, and then look away without ever touching it. Other days, I would pick it up multiple times, touch it and even attempt to read the summary, and again I would throw it under the desk.

What I began to notice was how I was feeling about going to work. I was excited and looked forward to seeing the book even if I wasn't committed to reading it. I even wondered how I would feel if it was suddenly gone. Oh and let's not forget my thoughts of taking the book home as I attempted to justify to myself why it wouldn't be a big deal.

I was out and about with one of my children at Barnes and Noble not looking for anything in particular, and that's the catch. You see, we don't have to look for it, we need only ask, and it will reveal itself to us when we are ready to receive it. The same book that was under my desk was right in front of me, and you bet your ass I bought it!

Ask and It Is Given is the writings of Abraham through a woman by the name of Esther Hicks who I didn't know much about other than my brother Dennis' continuous suggestion to read it. He believed that many of the questions I had regarding purchasing the book were more for symbolism than anything else. In fact, I don't believe I've read an entire chapter, and the book is in mint condition. What I came to learn was the answers I had been seeking would be found within and not outside of me.

The Last Fight

My duties were to make sure everyone, staff inmates, medical staff, and professional visitors, was safe by maintaining the peace and making sure everyone behaved. I was the eyes and ears along with whomever my partner was if I had one to make sure nothing was brought into or removed from the clinic without permission.

I often had other officers come hang out with me. Some were having issues either at home, work or they wanted to be heard and seen. I had, in a sense, created a space for many to come and let go without fear that it would go anywhere else. They trusted my suggestions and the advice I would give. My guess is most officers and staff, in general, could see I was fair and tended to have an open mind about it all even when surrounded by negativity.

As I began my day, something was different. It was one of those "listen to your gut" days, and I found it a little odd because I was feeling pretty good after my morning cardio session. As the inmates arrived, I checked off the names as the escorting officer opened the holding cell door which was a waiting room for the inmates until they were called to be seen by medical staff.

One of the women instantly caught my attention, and I knew in my gut if there was going to be a problem it would be with her. I was not familiar with this inmate; she didn't appear to be one of our regulars. Her demeanor gave me the impression that she was familiar with law enforcement and I sensed she could have been in custody perhaps in another county jail.

I sized her up immediately. She was a black female about 5'7", 220 lbs. but with a stocky build, so she didn't look it, which meant she was mad strong. We were both sporting a TWA (teenie weenie afro's), so it was a given that there wasn't going to be any hair pulling or scratching. This was going to be a boxing match, a freaking takedown, and I knew she was going to give me a run for my money as the fight or flight switch automatically shifted into the "on" position.

The first couple of times I walked back to the holding cell, I unlocked the door and called the name of another inmate. She would stare at me and roll her eyes in disgust and mumble something under her breath. As I walked back to my desk, I could feel it again and I knew shit was going to hit the fan, but I was trying my best.

I returned an inmate back to the cell who had been seen. I called another inmate out and it wasn't her. As the inmate walked out and the door began to shut, I heard her call me a bitch. Instantly, the air was crispy, and I went into my "Oh no she didn't!" but I managed to stay focused on what I was doing. The tension was thick. You could cut it with a knife, and the inmates in the holding cell began to make room just in case we threw down.

As the door shut, I could hear some of the other inmates attempt to defend me. I heard them asking her "Why are you tripping? Ms. Shaviri is cool she's one of the nice officers," and I hear a couple of other ones say, "She ain't the one man, I wouldn't fuck with her!"

I returned another inmate and called for a different one. I knew I couldn't wait any longer. I needed to remove the inmate before she created a larger problem in the holding cell. As she stepped up to the door and demanded to be seen, she stated how long she'd been waiting and angrily said, "Fuck you, bitch." I said, "What did you just call me?" (I know right? I heard her loud and clear.) She replied with, "You heard me." The other inmates froze with big eyes that looked like question marks as they backed up and waited for the next move.

I decided it would be best to separate her from the other inmates by placing her in a single holding cell until the medical staff was ready to see her. I opened the main holding cell door and motioned to her to step out of the cell. As I escorted her down the hall, I walked behind her on the right. Suddenly, she turned towards me, and before I knew it, I was doing a flying ninja move. No, not really, but I do remember her coming towards me, grabbing her arm, us spinning round and round. From the moment I put my hands on her, I could hear the alarms going off in my head because she was as strong as an ox. I heard this voice saying, "Ride 'em, cowboy. You better not let her go because if you do, she is gonna whip yo ass," so I held on tight.

We were standing near the office of one of the psychologists. I planted her face into the window and managed to get one of her arms behind her back. As I verbally directed her to give me her other hand, she refused. One of the many skills I learned growing up in Chicago that has helped me tremendously over the years of working in the jail was the importance of paying attention to detail. Yes, eye contact, body language, being fair, firm and consistent were key, but that gut feeling automatically sends you on high alert, and you just know you need to be on your toes.

Going from professional to physical was not always in a day's pay, but it was always a part of the job. We went from standing at the window to suddenly doing a shot-put spin to landing hard my right knee jammed into the cement floor. She was face down with her arm beneath her body still refusing to comply with my directive to place it behind her back. I applied pressure behind her left ear thinking it would cause her to comply, but she didn't even flinch. I am fucking screaming, "HELP!!! SOMEBODY HELP ME!!!" in my head. It was a challenge to press the key of my radio to call for assistance.

I was ready to be done with this, so I let go of the arm on her back and quickly pressed the key on the mic of my radio which was near the collar of my uniform, and with lightning speed, officers responded. Thank goodness, because I was exhausted, but you wouldn't have known it because I wouldn't let anyone see me sweat.

I had managed to get through nearly twenty years without any major injury, and I definitely did not want to add one that day.

As I sat down to write the report, there was an incredible amount of laughter within me. Two women in their middle to late forties had a physical altercation, a fight, a rumble. I was 48 and she was 46 years old. The more I thought about it, the more I laughed until my eyes watered. It was downright hilarious.

Although we are trained to apply various levels of force, there are times when that goes out the window. Sure, I'd had many encounters similar to this one throughout my career, but this one was different. Now, do you want to talk about a sign or clue? This one was a clear message to be aware of and receptive to what came next.

Big Magic At Costco

October 5, 2015

I found myself being apprehensive to share most of my experiences, even with some of my closest friends, and even more so when it came to my husband and children. I was that friend that dared to step outside of the box, eager to try something new and adventurous. The difference this time was, had I gone too far?

I was a wife, mom, friend, motivator, and confidant to many who was supposed to know what to do when something like this happened. How could I share what was happening with someone else, and more importantly, who did I feel comfortable enough to share it with? There was also an underlying fear within, although faint, of someone close to me suggesting that I seek professional help because they were worried about me.

My cup was full internally and I knew it, yet I remained open to something I had difficulty explaining to others, like the day I was led to my neighborhood Costco. Have you ever had the feeling that your body was moving but your mind was without thought? Have you ever thought about something that happened and you can't remember consciously going there? My world had begun to change so rapidly I could hardly keep up. I could think a thought, and it would manifest within a matter of weeks. The more that I tuned into them, the quicker they would appear.

I can remember a sudden yet faint urge to leave my home. It was like I was supposed to go somewhere or do something, and it made me uneasy. It was quite fascinating at how it worked initially, yet, quite overwhelming at times. It was like knowing something was about to happen but not really knowing, but detaching just enough from the need to have an immediate understanding and being fully aware of the magical moment when it took place.

As I reflect back on this particular event, I can remember standing in the entryway of the kitchen. I found myself breathing in kind of a rhythmic flow for several breaths. I remember picking up my keys, and slipping my cross-body purse over my head when leaving the house.

Costco? Yes. I showed my membership card, entered and walked in the direction of the books. That's when I saw the book! It not only took my breath away, but it made me jerk. The cover was an array of vibrant living colors; it was blue, fuchsia, with a splash of yellow. I touched it as if it was a secret treasure patiently waiting for me to discover it.

As I slowly caressed the cover, I whispered the title just loud enough for my ears to hear it: "*Big Magic: Creative Living Beyond Fear.*" As I picked it up, my heart danced. I decided it was a keeper and headed towards the checkout, but not before grabbing a package of chocolate-covered almonds.

As I exited the store, it felt as if I was almost being carried back to my car, moving without any effort of my own. I began to feel like a kid again, full of joy and excitement. It was like nostalgically playing with a new toy or going to a special place with one of your siblings or someone you loved dearly, but this time it was the anticipation of opening up a book. I opened the door and sat in the driver's seat. I placed the package of almonds in the passenger seat. As I opened the book and read the first few lines, I could feel the tears rolling down my cheeks and the sound of my heartbeat in my ears. I was hitting the steering wheel and shouting, "Yes, yes, yes! I'm not crazy! Yes!" Before long, I found myself sobbing and laughing at the same time. As I wiped my eyes and looked up through the windshield of my car, I hoped the customers walking through the parking lot had not noticed me. "Freakin aye! There's nothing wrong with me!!!" This was me. I could totally relate to what was being communicated through the pages of that book. It's like it was meant for me to have! I clearly knew what the writer was talking about because I've experienced some of this! This is the shit that I couldn't talk to many people about because they would've thought I was crazy, but I'm not! Then I thought, "If I was crazy, the person that wrote this book had to be crazy too!" which totally made sense to me.

I decided to try and compose myself enough to find out who the writer was in between blowing my nose and wiping my tears, and there it was clear as day on the front cover, but I never got past "Big Magic." It was a gal by the name of Elizabeth Gilbert who was the same author of *Eat, Pray, Love* and I guess several other books. I have to admit I didn't know much about her, but I had heard of the movie that Julia Roberts was in where she played to role of a lady who was trying to find herself and it was surrounded by her effort in eating, praying and loving everyone.

In any case, my life began to feel like it was spinning out of control. It was scary, but it was great! Daily, I began to feel an incredible amount of joy like never before. In fact, I could hardly wait to wake up in the morning to experience what the day held for me. I found it fascinating to think about something, and even if it didn't go the way I wanted it to go, there was always an even better outcome with patience and awareness.

The greatest challenge was, I was the only one in my household who was experiencing this new-found awareness, and it became uncomfortable rather quickly. I felt isolated, excluded. I wondered if I still belonged at home. I struggled to explain what was happening to my family, but it was as if I was speaking Spanish and they could only understand English. There was clearly a communication barrier, but I continued to believe it would all work out.

Trust The Unknown

October 23, 2015

I'd been a Corrections Deputy for the County Sheriff's Department for over two decades, and for the most part, it wasn't a terrible place to work. It had its moments like any job or career. Every day was a grab bag kind of day, and the only consistent thing was your attitude going in and the uniform, but over the last year, something had begun to shift.

That feeling that I spoke about earlier on? Well, it was there even as I applied for a position with the county, but I didn't get it, I mean I did and didn't. You see, I wanted to open up a cafe in downtown Tacoma, Washington. Yes, quite a contrast to working in a jail. The call came through with the hiring offer for the county, and after discussing it with my husband, I accepted the job. That feeling continued to come to me in a variety of ways. When the thought of leaving entered my mind, I would shut it down thinking to myself, "There's no way I can quit my job." I had one child when I began working for the department, and now I had three, and that was an incredible amount of responsibility.

I wanted to sit down and talk to my husband about how I was feeling, but simply didn't want the fight or argument about how irrational it would be to quit. Also, I don't think I was ready all those times before. It would have taken a lot of courage and strength to follow through, and I still had some work to do. In fact, I was very grateful for my husband's responses and trust in me when I say he could be a major jerk (my thinking then). In time, he would turn out to be one of the best teachers (I have told him that more times than I can remember).

Because I wasn't sure if leaving the job was the right thing to do, I stayed. It was easy, I knew the work like the back of my hand, it came with great benefits, an amazingly dysfunctional work family, and it paid well—but it came with a price. That invisible presence never disappeared; it remained right there watching and waiting patiently for me to step into who I was becoming.

I'm Out

I went into work like I would on a normal day. I didn't go in thinking today was going to be my last day as an officer. After all, I hadn't spoken to anyone seriously about leaving, which was not a decision that I had made at that point—or, had I? There was no letter of resignation written, I had not spoken to human resources or my supervisor. Hell, I don't even remember telling my two best friends about it.

I could remember cleaning my work area over several days, almost as if I was preparing myself for the birth of something. It was like that of an expectant mother who suddenly cleans the house from top to bottom in preparation for her child's arrival into the world. I was preparing myself for birth or rebirth of my life! This realization brings so much more clarity to me, even in this moment.

After lunch, I could feel it again, that feeling I now refer to as “the nudge.” It had been growing over the last few days. There was a message that was being delivered to me: it was time to go, trust; you must go. The message also made it clear, that if you do not adhere to this calling something terrible may happen, or you will miss something incredible. It was a message that came to me as clear as day, and it was all relayed through a feeling.

I agreed to trust and go with it. I had absolutely no fear whatsoever! I knew it was all going to work out somehow. I let go. I was ready! I believed in something that I could not see or touch that would lead me to where I needed to go. I left on a Friday, and it turned out to be one of the best weekends I have had in a very long time, one of liberation, peace, and sheer joy! I told one of my two best friends I was done, and I wouldn’t be returning, but I don’t think she believed me in the beginning. My husband didn’t even know I had left for nearly two weeks after. When he found out, he completely exploded, turning red and running around the house in circles, but it didn’t faze me at all by then. I looked at him, smiled and assured him that it was all going to be okay. “I’m going to take care of us in time, not sure how, but I just know that I am,” I said. He shook his head and walked away. I was sure he was thinking I had lost my mind. All I could do was smile and tell myself that it was going to all work out.

From that moment on, there have been good days and not so good days. I felt really bad knowing my husband was carrying the weight of our household on his shoulders financially. I understood more than he realized that his need to make sure all we've worked for over the past couple of decades didn't go down the drain due to me walking away from my career and my inability to give him any concrete answer regarding a plan of action on my part. I just didn't know what the next step would be and it seemed as if every time I placed a timetable or deadline to prove to my family that I was on track, the clues, signs, messages would suddenly slow down, and some days they wouldn't even show up.

I was grateful for it all and would imagine some folks that would've simply walked away and called it "quits," but I believe in his own way he wanted to see us make it through. Still, I believed with every cell in my body that there was something far greater in store for my family and it would be beyond anything they could possibly imagine.

I've been told by many what a courageous thing it was to leave my job. I was even asked how it felt and if I was afraid and was my husband happy about it? It was a little challenging to explain, and I often had difficulty describing it without sounding as if I was a nut job. As always, the words "it was a feeling and knowing within" inevitably would roll off my tongue.

It's All Beautiful

I hadn't felt so alive in years. It was like I was suddenly in love with life itself. I noticed everything around me, and it was beautiful! I would find myself running on the same trail I'd been running on for years noticing all of the little things that I hadn't previously. The trees suddenly were green, not just the color green, like a crayon. They were a vibrant, living, breathing green. I would often feel the rush of gratitude fill me up with joy just because I was able to see it.

I remember once I was running, and although there are dog poop bags at the beginning and end of the trail, sometimes folks forget or don't bother to grab a couple to stick in their pocket to scoop the poop. When the doggies poop on the trail, sometimes that is where it's left. I was running, and that joy of being alive hit me. I was dancing, singing, skipping as though I was about six or seven years old. I noticed a pile of dog poop on the trail, and when I say pile, it's a pile. Anyway, I stop in my tracks and just looked at it. I was simply in awe, thinking of how beautiful it was. It was quite the creation, and it was a deep, rich mahogany brown. Even with all of the bumps, bruises, sideswipes, and attempted roadblocks, I continued on. I asked myself every now and again if I was going too far, and before I could finish the question, I knew…I knew I was exactly where I was supposed to be.

Ready Or Not

November. 2015

I found myself sitting in my sage Toyota Highlander feeling completely lost and confused. I began to talk to myself quietly as if I someone else would hear me, "What the hell was going on with me?" I was the only one in the car at 4:45am! Still, I couldn't get past the feeling that there was something I was supposed to understand, do or be, but I was having a difficult time making any sense of it.

I decided to call my sister, Debbie, who although we didn't see eye to eye during our teen and young adult years. We began to get closer as I graduated from high school and after I went away to college. Debbie became more of an elder or one that could help ground me when I would find myself bouncing off the wall full of ideas on how to change the world. She listened attentively, without interruption and you knew you mattered, and your issues weren't just a broken record; they were important. What was super cool was that whatever I thought I was struggling with at the time, she rarely ever told me what to do. But she had a way of responding by reflecting back to you what she believed you had shared using her words and you could see multiple solutions. She was open to listening to what I was experiencing, and she really wanted to help me get through the struggle I was having in my mind. We'd grown to like one another over the years, but not so much when we were younger.

I'd talk to her about the coincidences that had taken place in Chicago when I was there for Patricia's funeral, and I know she believed me. Can you imagine thinking a thought about something that you wanted or interested you and—voila—there it was? Sometimes immediately, no not always immediately, but eventually, it became a physical reality.

My sense of awareness was like that of a sleeping giant who decided it was time to wake up from its nearly half-century slumber. It was simply me tuning in to my vibration with the Universe and life itself. It was the realization of my connection to all things living. This is what it felt like to be present.

I began each day with a knowing that when my eyes opened, with no doubt in my mind, I was going to experience something magical, even with all of the contrast that was bound to come my way. In time, I began to feel as if I had learned a new language. I could understand what the laws of the universe were and how they worked, what words like vibration, frequency, and energy meant. The ability to go beyond bullshit surface vibes by seeing through them with love and connection was blowing my mind. As I continued to fine tune my awareness of it all, I could sense when someone was not in a good space, and their energy was not well to include my own. I was learning to reconnect to a gift that had been there all along but lay buried beneath my prior learnings which began to shatter.

As Debbie and I talked, I found myself beginning to cry because I didn't understand why my life was changing so rapidly, and in a direction that I was not familiar with. I told her that all I wanted was to understand it. I shared with her that I knew I wasn't crazy, but there was clearly something that was being placed before me that was causing me great distress because I just wasn't getting it.

As the tears continued to flow down my face like the raw, rapid wave of a wild river, I struggled to breathe. I felt a slowly increasing lump in the center of my throat and the death grip of cocoa knuckles began to turn white from squeezing the steering wheel. My entire body suddenly became paralyzed with tremendous fear. I had thoughts of my inability to gain a clear understanding, or some form of control as to what was happening. If I could only have something or someone let me know that I'm not losing my mind and it would be okay, eventually I would have a sense of relief. I could feel the helplessness of my sister through the phone as she let out a sigh. She then asked me if there was any way I could get away. She asked if there was a place in my home where I could be alone. I told her the best place was my walk-in closet, but that was about it. She asked if I could get away for a short time, and I could feel the panic setting in. Suddenly it dawned on me that I was registered for the Las Vegas Rock & Roll Half Marathon which was less than two weeks out. I immediately felt a shift from feeling confused and utter loss to a thought of being alone with the opportunity to calm my mind.

As I reached for the handle to open the door of my SUV, I felt an onset of sheer fear and panic. I was crying profusely, and I felt like I couldn't breathe. I had a death grip on the steering wheel, and I couldn't stop crying. My phone rang, and it was my brother Dennis. I answered it as I mentally told myself to be cool and not let him know what just happened.

Dennis: "How's you?"

Me: "I'm good."

Dennis: "Yeah?"

Me: "Yep."

Dennis: "You sure?"

Me: (Sobbing) "I don't know what's wrong with me Dennis."

Dennis: "Oh yeah? What's the problem?"

Me: "I…I'm scared Dennis. Dennis. I'm scared."

Dennis: "Oh yeah? Why are you scared? I mean, what scares you? Did something happen?"

Me: "I think I'm about to blow up, Dennis."

Dennis: "Oh yeah, okay. Blow up how? Where are you right now?"

Me: (Still crying) "I'm sitting in my truck in the driveway."

Dennis: "Okay. So you said that you think you are about to blow up; blow up how?"

Me: (sobbing heavier) "People are going to know me."

Dennis: "Okay, so, I'm still confused. You are afraid of blowing up because you think people are going to know you? But, don't people know you now? You have your husband, children, coworkers, friends and many others that know you."

With my brother's last question, I could immediately feel a sense of calm, but I was still a bit anxious.

Me: "I don't know if that's what I want, Dennis."

Dennis: "What do you mean? You don't want people to know you? What don't you want?"

Me: "I mean people are really going to know me. I don't know if I want all of that. I like my life now."

Dennis: "When you say you think you are about to blow up, people are going to know you, are you talking about know you like, umm, some sort of celebrity, or someone famous? Like you could be on the cover of a magazine or on TV or something?"

I started crying heavily again because my brother hit the nail on the head. I could feel a change was taking place and it was a knowing that I was going to be eventually surrounded by people, outside of those whom I'd known for more than half my life, and it terrified me.

My brother thought it was exciting. In fact, he gave a little giggle once he understood what I was talking about. He told me that it would be alright, and I was just getting ready for the next level, and he believed everything that was happening was a result of something I asked for from the Universe/Source, and now I was ready to see it come to life. The problem was that I had no clue what I'd asked for or agreed to. In time, it would reveal itself in an ever-changing way. He assured me, and I believed him. I listened to my brother a bit longer and suddenly felt extremely exhausted, completely drained. We agreed to talk later. I went into the house, sat on the sofa with a blanket and went to sleep.

The Island

Nov. 6, 2015

It had been coming on for a while, but I continued to push it away and tried desperately to avoid it altogether. My husband and I were continuing to drift apart as the arguments increased, all due to my challenge to communicate my next step when it came to helping our family financially. I felt like a lost puppy in the middle of an intersection, desperately trying to find a way onto a path that would provide a sense of safety, and above all else, silence.

I knew something was happening, but I didn't know how to explain it to my husband and children. They too struggled to understand what was happening in their home. I could see the desperation in their eyes and the frustration in their interactions with me as they tried as best they could not to say something that would cause me to feel rejected or hurt my feelings. They were confused and wanted their mom back, and that wasn't going to happen. A shift of consciousness had occurred, and I couldn't go back to who I once was without enduring a tremendous amount of suffering, and I wouldn't go back if I could. I was alive, and it felt great!

I would like to say that it happened suddenly, but that wouldn't be true. You see, it was a feeling that I'd felt many times before, but I would push it away. When the thought of why am I here and there is something more I should be doing would arise, I would either laugh or scold myself at the thought of quitting my job. With all of the responsibilities that lay before my husband, I thought it would be a downright selfish move on my part. Also, there was a real possibility of my husband totally losing his mind.

I began to realize they didn't understand me. It was like we were on two different stations. A better example would be like when you listen to the radio and there is a song playing, but you can't quite make out what the sound is because there's a ton of static. After a while, you simply change the station, and now you can't hear any of the music that's playing.

The station I was on was suddenly changed, and no matter how much I tried to get back to my original station, I couldn't. The tune that was playing had changed, and another song was on.

It was my husband's fear of an unknown financial disaster that made me feel like I was being attacked because I would suddenly become tongue-tied each time he would ask me, "What are you going to do? Do you realize we have responsibilities? Do you have a plan or do you think something is just going to fall out of the sky?" Yes, of course, my feelings were hurt repeatedly. I didn't know how to explain what was happening with me, and each time I tried to share an experience with him, I would shut down.

My husband tended to see it all as black and white and kept it simple, but that wasn't the case through my eyes. He would share his thoughts of rationalization and probability any time I attempted to share some of my experiences, and I would simply shut down.

What I didn't realize was his feeling of helplessness for not being able to understand what was going on with me or simply wanting it to go away so we could get back to "normal," whatever that was anymore. My life had changed so drastically that my husband would warn me to be careful of "tampering with my mind" and even suggested that I not "think too much." I was beginning to wonder if he was right. Yeah, you read it. What the hell?

I would take it personally, and the opportunity for us to talk about anything became less and less. I would shut down and withdraw into my shell to protect myself from feeling attacked. It had been nearly two weeks since leaving my job on that Friday in October. Here stood the guy I had been married to for more than half my life, full of panic, and basically telling me he was afraid for my mental well-being. All I knew was, I couldn't return to jail. I clearly understood if I did not leave, something terrible was going to happen. Out of all of my years working at the jail, I'd never felt that urge and understood the message before me so clearly.

Linda And The Blue SUV

November 2015

Yup, I had another one of those "A-ha!" growth moments today. One of the goals on my to-do list today was to have a mani/pedi along with changing my nose piercing. After browsing Groupon (yes, I'm always looking for a deal) and not being confident, I would be able to make an appointment to have the mani/pedi done before my departure on Friday, so I thought I would just take a pass.

For some reason, I couldn't just let the mani/pedi go though. Then I thought that I'll just try my luck at Paradise Nails and Spa. Usually, when I go there it's packed, but they managed to make the 15-minute wait actually a 15-minute wait. So, I arrived and went in. All chairs are full except one on the very end. I informed the woman that greeted me of the services I was looking for, and she told me it'd be about a 45-minute wait. I thanked her and I was off again. I then thought, "Screw the nails; just wear sneakers. It's not like it's Spring or Summer. Go and change your piercing out."

I decided to go with Plan B: change my nose ring. I stopped by a nearby Walgreens to purchase a hair trimmer so that I wouldn't gross out the piercing artist as they changed my ring (because I'm too afraid). As I checked out, I asked the cashier if she could refer me to a salon nearby to have a manicure and pedicure. The cashier responded, "Believe it or not, a lot of us go to Wal-Mart, and they do a pretty good job." I thanked her, and I was off again, on a mission to get this goal of the day accomplished. I asked Google to direct me to the nearest Wal-Mart which was less than a couple miles from my current location, and I was in motion once again. As I got closer to my destination, I made a left turn on Marks Avenue, signaled and got into the left lane only to notice that the car in front of me had begun to slow down tremendously and then stop. Yup, you got it—out of gas. I was flustered because I'd been trying to get these two items checked off my list for some time now. So I waited until it was clear and merged into traffic just enough to go around the stalled vehicle and turn left at the immediate light.

Once the green arrow appeared, I began to turn left, only to have a blue SUV honk the horn like a mad person because I was turning as though it was a single turning lane when in fact it was two lanes. "Okay, Okay, I'm sorry 'bout that," I said out loud in my vehicle with my right hand up in an apologetic manner and quickly steered more to stay in my lane. As the vehicle passed, the woman inside was without a doubt calling me everything but a child of God. It wasn't until I clearly saw she'd called me a bitch that I felt disturbed. Then I noticed that she made a right into the Wal-Mart parking lot and I thought to myself, "I want to speak with her." Yeah, I know what you're thinking: "Who does that? Move on." But I just couldn't.

As I got out of the car, I found myself still thinking about the woman in the blue SUV. My eyes even began to sweep the parking lot for her vehicle, and then I had to ask myself, "What are you doing? Stop it." So, I let it go and took my thoughts back to the reason I was out and about, and that was to get a mani/pedi, finally. I stopped at the entrance of DaVita Nail Salon where I was told it would be about a 15-minute wait. I thought that was great—yes! I stopped by McDonald's and purchased a black cup of coffee and thought I'd kill some time just browsing around the store. I would every now and again think about the woman in the blue SUV and was bummed that I wouldn't have an opportunity to speak with her.

Anyway, I chose a line that appeared to be moving. One person was checking out and one was behind which would make me third in line. The woman at the front was quite the talker, and then I happened to notice that the cashier was a talker too, but I asked myself what the hurry was and began to relax about the wait. She was still there with another order she wanted to pay for separately (are you kidding me?).

Her transaction was finally complete, and she was moving. The fellow in front of me was kind. He placed an order divider in front of mine as well as for the guy behind me. My concern was, I would go back to the salon and find that I'd have to wait, but that's not what happened—yes! One of the technicians seated me in one of the pedicure chairs, and the magic was about to begin. As I placed my right then my left foot in the tub, a sense of peacefulness came over me. I thought to myself that it was unfortunate that the woman in the blue SUV allowed herself to become so angry with me to the point that she blew her top. Now I'm not saying that I was always cool about that stuff either, but over the last few years, I was aware of my temper in the car and I had to consciously tell myself to relax.

I decided to text my oldest daughter with a "Hello," and she hit me with a "Hi." Then I glanced to my right where I could see the last checkout. I immediately knew it was the lady in the SUV, although her windows were tinted and I couldn't see her face. But I could see the outline of her hair, and it appeared to be a natural afro. I knew it was her and thought how I would ever know. My feet were in this tub. What was I going to do, just break and run over there to the checkout? I thought to myself, "Okay Felicia, it's over, let it go. Why is it so important?" But I couldn't, and I didn't know why. I glanced over at her every now and then as she was checking out, and then we made eye contact. We both knew who the other was. She appeared to have a small child with her around three or four years of age.

Her transactions completed, she left the store, and I could no longer see her. Then I heard someone on the outside of the entrance say hello to some of the technicians. She was addressing them by name, so I gathered she frequently came to the salon. As she said hello to the tech that was working with me, I apologized for interrupting and asked her if she happened to be driving a blue SUV. She replied that she was, and immediately went into how I'd cut her off. I asked if she could pull her cart with her child near so that I could have a word with her, and she said, "Sure."

I told her that I hoped she would come into the store because I wanted to speak with her. I told her that I wanted to apologize for not being more aware of the traffic signal and I could clearly see she was livid. I held out my hand and introduced myself as Felicia Shaviri, and she told me her name was Linda. I informed her that I was from Seattle and I know some but not all of the streets in the area.

Linda went on to explain that she was afraid because she had her granddaughter in the car with her. She apologized for losing her cool and explained that it was just a reaction. I said, "No worries. It happens to the best of us." I apologized again for causing her quite the scare and wished her a good day.

This experience for me was more about the thought. It was about my wanting to speak with a complete stranger, one that I could only describe as having an afro because of the silhouette in her car. I didn't want to be tough or fight or tell her off. I truly wanted to meet her. When someone cuts me off, I may get a little upset, but if they throw their hands up or make an attempt to acknowledge a mistake, all is forgiven.

We've all been in this position before at one point or another during our years of driving. The next time you feel slighted no matter where you are, it can be anywhere, ask yourself how important it is to cuss that person out? How does it make you feel afterward? Was it worth your time and energy? Did they know they offended you? Press the pause button and simply walk it off. Most importantly, was there a lesson or connection for me through that experience? What was I supposed to get from that, and did I? Yes, this was one of those "God winks."

God Winked At Me

November 7, 2015

It was several days before I was to run in the Las Vegas Rock & Roll Marathon. I enjoyed registering for events ahead of time and then working my way towards accomplishing the goal. I was in a very different place this go-round than in all my years previous.

I flew to Vegas alone and would be staying at our home in Henderson. I arrived five days earlier just to get settled in and to have a little solitude. I decided to get out of the house and head towards one of the local malls. I went into one of the department stores meandered through not really in need of anything, simply killing some time and tired of being in the house.

Exiting the store, I glanced back towards the Barnes and Noble while walking towards my car and noticed a welcoming fellow sitting on a bench out front who looked like a "Farmer John" in his overalls, boots, beard, and tee.

There was a faint pull or push within that beckoned me to go into the store. But I thought about all of the books that I had at home already that I had yet to open. I immediately thought to myself, "Felicia, you don't need any more books. You need to read the books you have first." I agreed with myself, got in the car and returned home.

The very next day, I found myself parked in the same stall. I got out of the car, walked across the pedestrian walk and directly into the Barnes & Noble. As I entered the second set of double doors, I began to wonder why I was there. I didn't know what I needed from the bookstore, but I went in anyway.

I passed the first display table and went directly to the second one where I stopped and looked down. There was my answer to what I'd asked for, a book titled, *When God Winks at You: How God Speaks Directly to You Through the Power of Coincidence.* I wanted to scream out loud. I couldn't believe it, but I could, if you know what I mean. It was almost as if there was a bright yellow arrow that only I could see, pointing me in the direction to go.

Every story in that book was me, me, me, me! It was such a relief to know that I was not going mad or in need of any kind of prescription medication. I was so grateful for the ability to feel and listen to that invisible force within that led me exactly to where I was supposed to be.

This book would be the second of many I would be guided to for understanding and direction. I just needed to be aware of the feeling. Soon after, I found myself talking with strangers anywhere and everywhere, sharing my discovery about finding this book! Guess what? They had the book too! What made this book even more special was the author—Squire Rushnell. He's the creator of Schoolhouse Rock! Yeah! Yeah!! He taught us about Bill on Capitol Hill, remember? Okay, so maybe that doesn't ring a bell for you if your parents didn't turn you on to it or you were born after 1996. It was one of the best educational animation shows ever!

I was shifting and I could see and feel things before they happened. I was still in the process of understanding what was happening. It was like I could see it and feel it but was having some trouble holding on to it. As always, that was okay because I knew there was more to come.

When Your Doctor Calls In Sick (Screaming Match)

Dec 2015

It was nearly two months since the day I'd left my place of employment, and things were really heating up at home. There was an enormous cloud that loomed over our household. It was full of mixed emotions wrapped in fear and uncertainty which in turn created an atmosphere of chaos for all living within its walls.

This particular day, the kids had already left for school, and I was in the back office. My husband came to the door and asked, "Hey are you busy working on something?" I responded with, "No, I just got off a call with a client. What's up?" He then said, "I don't know what's going on with you, but I think we need to talk." I said, "Okay." I could tell from his tone of voice and body language that he was angry, but I told myself to stay cool.

He then began firing off questions at me like an automatic weapon. "What are your plans? Are you not going back to work? Are you quitting? Does the department know? What are you going to do? Were you planning on talking to me about this? We have three kids that we're responsible for that we need to provide for."

My response started out cool and I replied with, "No, I'm done. I won't be going back to work in the jail." He looked at me with big eyes. His face instantly turned red, and he asked, "Are you for real?" I calmly said, "Yes."

He then asked if I could just give it two more years and I said "No." He asked for a year, and I said "No." Six more months and I said, "No." Booooom!!! He exploded and began to shout and tell me how irresponsible I was and that quitting my job is completely selfish and self-centered. Next came, "How and why would I think it is okay to just up and quit your job with all of the responsibilities that we have? We have kids that we need to take care of! How are we supposed to pay for their college?! What are you thinking? Oh, I forgot, you're only thinking about yourself that's right, no one else in the family matters! All I'm asking you for is just a year! I'm trying to get us to a certain point to prepare for our retirement—a year, 12 months—and then I could care less if you sat on your ass for the rest of your life! I'm only asking for a year, and you can't even give me that!

Now it was my turn:

"You don't get it!! That place is killing me!!! It is killing my spirit!!! I am dying in there! Do you want a fucking year!? You got it!! I will go back to work for one fucking year and not a minute over, damn it!!! As a matter of fact, I have a doctor's appointment this afternoon at one. When I go there, I will tell Dr. G that I am good to go, to please sign the paperwork, so I can take my black ass back to work! Happy??? There, are you happy now???!!! Now, you'll have whatever you want, how about that? Have it your way! Done!! Can you please leave me alone now? I don't want to talk about this anymore. I'm done with this conversation. I'll be going back as soon as possible."

My husband looked relieved, yet there was a sense of sadness surrounding him. He tried to apologize for getting angry, but I wanted no part of it. I didn't want to hear anything he had to say. As I asked him to please leave me alone, my cell phone rang. I switched into gear and answered in that professional Siri voice.

Me: "Hello?"

Female: "Hello, may I speak to Felicia Shaviri?"

Me: "This is Felicia. Who's calling, please?"

Female: "Oh, Hi Felicia. This is Barbara from Dr. G's office."

Me: "Yes, hello Barb. How are you?"

Female: "I'm doing great, but unfortunately Dr. G isn't, and that's why I'm calling. You were scheduled to see him this afternoon at one, and because he wasn't feeling so well, he needs to clear his calendar for the day. I am so sorry about this."

Me: "Oh, no worries. I hope he feels better soon."

Female: "As do I. I can reschedule a later date with you now if you'd like or you can check your calendar and give us a call back."

Me: "Umm, how about I check my calendar and give you a call later in the week?"

Female: “Sounds good! Thank you for being so understanding, Felicia.”

Me: “No, thank you for calling to let me know.”

Female: “You are very welcome. Have a great day!”

Me: “Thank you, and you as well.”

After ending the call, I stood there stunned and wondered if my mind was playing tricks on me. I couldn’t help but think there was something so out of this world amazing that just happened and I couldn’t even share it with anyone that would believe it. I was done with all the tension in the house surrounding me. Quitting my job and that morning’s verbal altercation completely sent me over the edge.

There wasn’t a doubt in my mind that if I’d gone into that office on that particular day and time, I would’ve gone back to work. Now, I don’t know if you believe in divine intervention and I wasn’t sure about it myself, but that day completely had me sold. I’ve never in my lifetime heard of a doctor’s nurse calling his patients because he wasn’t feeling well, but I’m sure glad that she did.

A Night at the Loft with Adele & Erin

(12-29-15)

Being a girl, it seems like the natural thing to do is to want to shop—not for me. It is a total drag. My daughters typically help me when it comes to dressing with a bit more “oomph” being 40 plus, and I must admit that for the most part, they’ve done fairly well.

Mica and I decided to get out of the house, unlike the fellas, and go for a walk around The District in Henderson. The District is a pretty cool, classy, boutique style shopping area. In any case, we wander into The Loft/Ann Taylor, and to both of our surprises they are having (you got it) an awesome *sale*! I go through and pick out several items that catch my eye, and Micah finds an item or two that she thinks would be flattering on me as well.

We're greeted by the sales attendant (Erin), and I ask what the return policy is and explain that I'm not big on shopping and I really wasn't in the mood to try anything on. The attendant explains and expresses that she completely understands and shared that she too dreads trying items on from time to time.

Well, Micah and I continued to shop around the store a bit more and then I expressed to her that I think I was done and I was ready to vamoose. Just to explain a bit more regarding my exhaustion with the shopping thingy: If I have a need to buy a certain item, I'll generally go to the mall with one of my daughters. In my mind, I want to get in and out, and I am seriously hoping that I can walk into the store and what I'm looking for will just pop right out in front of me, mission accomplished, and I can now depart—*not*!

Generally, I can manage 30-45 minutes in a department store, and then it hits me, and I'm *done*! My tolerance of people and their callousness when it comes to shopping is minimal. I don't like the fact that someone could drop an item on the floor and not pick it up or step over an item. I don't care for the desperation, rudeness and disregard for others all because so many people are wrapped up in themselves and trying to get that item that will outdo the Jones's.

Okay, back to The Loft:

While checking out, the cashier (Adele) asked if we wanted to donate to St. Jude's and I politely declined and explained our family donates to charities throughout the year and not just during the holiday season. She stated that she understood and elaborated that The Loft has been part of the St. Jude Foundation for about 12 years which I thought was pretty impressive. Adele informed us about the challenges the employees at the store would set at the beginning of the day and that hers for the day was $20 and she believed she was at $18.50. The neat thing about Adele was that she didn't ask twice nor pressured us, although the chances of a customer coming in and donating were growing slimmer because the shop was going to be closing soon.

I mentioned to her that I thought they had some great sales. I told her that I was looking to change my look from my normal comfort clothes to more of an age-appropriate classic and fun look.

She immediately knew what I was looking for and introduced me to the Lois & Gray line which is a chic sportswear line that I completely loved! She suggested that I check online for more of a selection and thought I would look great in that line, and although I didn't try a single item on, I couldn't agree more.

We thanked her and began to leave the shop, but there was another rack that caught our eye where we picked a couple more items, and upon completing the second purchase, added that $1.50 to Adele's tally and "ding" went the bell. I went on to share with her some of the many experiences that I've been having over the past few years and told her some of the stories like "Road Rage with Linda". By this time, Erin had joined us and both were completely engaged in what I was sharing. I told them that I was on the verge of taking a huge leap by making a career change and that it was actually in motion as we spoke.

Erin asked what I did, and I told her I was a Corrections Deputy in Washington State and had been for over 20 years. Erin then shared that her mother had retired nearly six years ago as a dispatcher and she stated her mom was having a challenge with not being able to manage people as she had been used to doing for so many years. When she asked me if I thought I would find that challenging, I responded very confidently that I did not believe so because there was another purpose for me. I told them both that I wasn't really sure where I was going to land, but that I truly felt like the road that I was on and the direction that I was going in was just where I was supposed to be.

Adele asked me if I was into the arts. I asked her to elaborate, she then went on to talk about writing and said that she was getting goosebumps as she listened to my story and thought I would be a great writer. She said she loved my storytelling and looked forward to the release of my book. I hadn't really thought about writing a book until nearly two years after meeting her.

Connection @FullLine
Wanted: Female Speakers

October. 16, 2016
Meeting Doris

It's truly interesting the way the doors of our lives open once we learn to slow down and truly appreciate life and all of the wonderful things that are taking place within and around us.

About three weeks ago, I was sitting on the loveseat in my home when a call came through from my eldest daughter, Jasmine. She sounded a bit disturbed and uneasy about something. I asked her if she was okay and she hesitated then responded. I was struggling, trying to keep my cool, but I really wanted to shout out, "SPIT IT OUT JASMINE!!!"

She finally began to speak, but not without pausing and saying, "Wow" and "Umm." She essentially told me about something that had just happened to her and how she immediately thought of me.

Jasmine is the last of my children to be present with me during any of my "more than a coincidence" moments. She told me about a woman that came into Nordstrom's, and it appeared she was looking for a handbag. Jasmine asked her if she needed any help and the woman responded by introducing herself as a writer, radio personality and entrepreneur in the area. She then reached into her tote and pulled out one of her books to show and handed Jasmine a business card. What Jasmine didn't know at the time was that she would be the connection that would lead to several more.

Jasmine sent me a photo of her business card, and I contacted her immediately. We spoke on the telephone for nearly two hours, and it was amazing. We had so much in common that we could hardly wait to meet. Doris, a radio personality in Lakewood, Washington, invited me to be a guest on her Sunday platform where we spoke about stepping outside of your comfort zones and trusting in yourself. We both shared the importance of taking chances and the importance of believing that you can, in fact, create the life that you desire. I knew she was in my life for a reason and I had the feeling more was to come.

Not long after the radio segment, I found myself in a studio recording Doris's autobiography, *The Reason Why.* I not only loved her story, but found myself laughing and crying several times while in the process of recording. Doris had a heart of gold and I was truly honored to be the voice of her story. Over the past several months, I learned not to try figuring out why someone crossed paths with me. Feeling there was more to come, I found myself saying "thank you" more often than normal and being open to whatever appeared.

October 19, 2016:

Doris asked me if I would like to go to a seminar in Seattle that would be offering information for female motivational speakers. Without hesitation, I told her I would check it out and asked when and what time. She informed me that it was on Wednesday, October 19, 2016 at the Crowne Plaza and it would be an all-day event from 9 a.m. – 4 p.m. and suggested that we carpool.

Needless to say, I agreed. We then communicated back and forth about carpooling. We knew it would be during the morning rush hour, so we wanted to find a location that would allow us to quickly hop back on I-5.

I woke up at 3:45 a.m. and read a message from Doris stating that she was not able to sleep during the night because she was so excited about going to the seminar. The feeling was mutual.

The plan was for them to pick me up at the Commons Mall in Federal Way, WA around 6:45 a.m. I get out of bed, put on the workout gear that I'd laid out the night before and hit the garage for some cardio. Somehow or another, I lost track of time and was running like a mad woman to get showered and dressed so that I would not be the one holding everyone up, causing the group to be late.

I was running around the house like a chicken with her head cut off. Thank goodness I'm easy to dress for the most part and low maintenance when it comes to the hair. Yup, I will be the first to admit there is nothing that comes close to sporting a TWA (teenie weenie afro), add water and watch it pop! Love it!

I hop in the car and go to the Commons Mall which is less than five miles from my home. Even then, I am struggling not to go into panic mode because I'm running a little bit behind, nearly 10 minutes from our agreed time of pickup.

I texted Doris to let her know that I was at the mall near Target. She called to let me know they will be leaving shortly after a quick stop at Starbucks. I responded by saying, "Okay, no worries. I'm going to run over to grab a cup of coffee from McDonald's, and I'll see you guys when you get here." I ended the call and begin laughing as I visualized the panic state I was in thinking I would be the late one.

The nearest McDonald's was about half a block away, if that. I decide not to go through the drive-thru because it could take a lot longer than expected. I parked, grabbed my phone and walked across the lot and into the restaurant. As I walk in, I noticed a young man who looked to be in his mid to late twenties looking at me. He would look at me, make eye contact and then turn away several times as if he was a shy teenage boy. I stepped closer to the register and requested a large cup of black coffee.

"Hello," I say to him, he nervously responds with a, "H-h-hi" and appeared to be a bit surprised and really not sure if I was speaking to him.

He gave me the impression that he was either a bit delayed, super shy or accustomed to not being seen. For some reason, I found myself being drawn to him enough to initiate a conversation.

I began by asking him why he was up so early in the morning and if he'd had breakfast. He said he'd put in an application and was checking back on the job (at 7:12 in the morning?). So, I must say I thought that reflected a person wanting to work and I offered to buy him breakfast. No, seriously I did.

Me: "Hey have you had breakfast yet?"

Mr: "Who…me?"

Me: "Duh, no, the other guy who's not standing next to you. Yes, you. Have you eaten this morning?"

Mr: "Uh…naw."

Me: "Can I buy you breakfast? Are ya hungry? I'd like to buy you breakfast."

He was looking at me like he couldn't believe I was insisting on buying breakfast for him. It was very transparent. The wheels were spinning, and he could not wrap his brain around why this lady who he didn't know and never saw before would insist on buying him breakfast.

Me: "Okay, now if you want me to buy you breakfast you gotta hurry up. I ain't got all day."

Mr: "Oh, okay, umm, umm, can I, umm, can I have a milkshake?"

Me: "A what?"

Mr: "Can I have a milkshake?"

Me: "Uhh, No. You ain't having a milkshake for breakfast. Who do you know has a milkshake for breakfast? I'll buy you some food but not a milkshake."

Mr: "Oh okay, so I shouldn't have a milkshake, huh?"

Me: “Nope.”

Then it hit me: who am I to tell someone what they can and cannot have? If you offer to treat someone to a meal, there should not be a limitation of what items they are allowed to have, within reason, of course.

So I offered an apology to this young man and encouraged him to order as he wished. I told him to order his milkshake if that’s what he would like to have for breakfast. He was looking at me totally confused at that point, and had a look on his face that was just like my Auntie Joyce.

Because the ice-cream dispenser was not up and running, the next closest item was a Mocha Frappe, of sorts. The cashier request four dollars and change and I looked at this young man and said, “Seriously? My coffee was only a dollar and ten cents.” Argh.

He gave a nervous smile, and I returned a heart-warming smile and told him that once he got this job, he had better hold on to it. I advised him that when he found himself getting irritated by his coworkers that he takes a deep breath to gather himself and say “this is small stuff” and that was to include our current cashier. I wished him a good day and best wishes on his journey. I turned and walked away never looking back at him, but I could feel both of them watching me as I exited.

After leaving the jail, I found myself slowly becoming less judgmental of others and more willing to help others. It’s not like I never did anything nice, donated to a charity or simply gave to another just to give. This was different. It was like I wanted to know how others were doing. If someone walked past me I would not only greet them, but I would often ask them how they were doing, and I would wait for their response which would catch them off guard because they probably didn't think I really wanted to know, but I did. I would eventually realize it was all part of something greater in the years to come.

I returned to the parking lot of the mall and parked at the end. I sat there for an additional twenty minutes or so. I could feel a bit of angst settling in as I began to question myself for depending on another person to drive me where I could've driven myself. Why didn't I just drive myself? It was freaking cold in that car, and my toes were starting to get numb. Argh…sigh. A Mercedes pulled up beside me, and there was a sense of relief. Although we were going to be late, it wouldn't be more than a quarter past. I got out of my car and noticed there were four women in the vehicle already. I hoped they wouldn't notice how my eyes got big as I attempted to wrap my head around the question, "How the heck am I supposed to get in there? And, if I do, what kind of tool would they need to pry me out?"

We hit the road and I thought I was going to die several times, but I know someone had to be watching over us all, especially all of the cars around us. It was the most hilarious and fascinating carpool I've ever been in. The language that was being spoken was that of Panamanian, Hebrew and good old fashioned English. I would have loved to be able to tell you what the topic was, but my mind was on "not dying."

We arrived, parked and entered the hotel. The seminar had already begun, so we tried to enter as quietly as possible. As we found our seats, one of the women said my name. There was a woman I was moving in front of who stopped me and said, “Felicia?” I said, “Yes?” It was one of my former coworkers. I hadn’t seen her in years, but she looked great and I was happy for her. She looked happy.

Less than ten minutes into listening to the seminar speaker, I was pissed! I found myself so irritated that I was struggling not to call him on his bullshit in front of the entire crowd. I scanned the audience who appeared to be mid-30s to retirement age. On their faces, you could see the desperation and hope of this being the golden ticket they’ve been waiting for to leave them from all of their financial woes. There was no doubt in my mind there were people planted in the audience to get the ball rolling for others to hop on board.

The final straw for me was when he began to show photos with celebrities like 50 Cent, and Damien somebody from Shark Show. I could feel myself becoming more angry and I was taking it personally and not it a good way. I decided this wasn’t a healthy environment for me when I got a visual of myself cussing this guy out. I knew there was a possibility of it going downhill fast. I could see it, me getting kicked out, arrested or both for causing a public disturbance.

I turned my focus to the women I arrived with, and I became concerned about what they would think of me. Would they think I was nuts because I could clearly see this guy was bullshit? Or better yet, what was the big deal and I why did I care so much? Maybe they could see it too, but it wasn’t as important, so I decided to let it go as well.

I decided it was best to excuse myself by informing the women that I needed to stretch my legs. I walked toward the back of the room and headed over towards the entrance, where I stood and continued to listen. I couldn't help but wonder how this dude was, without effort, pulling the wool over the eyes of more than half of the audience. The urge came back to shout out, but I decide to step out into the hall and away for some fresh air. I guess I thought it would allow me to clear my head and get grounded.

Powder Room Connection

I stood in the lobby for several minutes, still feeling some angst about what I believed was a waste of my time. I decided to go to the ladies room. As I entered, I found two or three women on their cell phones googling this guy. I gave a little chuckle as I said to them, "So I'm not the only one who thinks this guy is bogus, huh?" One of them responded with, "No this guy is a scam artist" and she shared some of what she found online about him.

As we stood there sharing our thoughts, another woman entered the ladies room bumping one of the two women with the door. She apologized and asked, "Oh, is this where the party is?" and the room filled with laughter. She said hello to me and asked how I was doing, and I said that I was pissed and about to give her an earful when she asked me to hold that thought because she really did need to use the bathroom.

After she came out, she washed her hands then came over to me and asked if I was okay. I responded with "Yes and no" and smiled at her. She asked that I continue. So, I began to fire off about how this guy was wasting my time, and I could be dead in the next ten minutes, but I've given him half of them. This guy was a scam artist, and he's going to get all of those people's money, and that's not right, etc.

She then placed her right hand on my left, and I got goosebumps that felt almost electric and traveled from my wrist to my shoulder. I said, “Wow,” and she apologized for shocking me. She asked me a question as she simultaneously placed her right hand on my left hand and again I got goosebumps. I went on to say, “This is pretty freaky.” I paused to allow a moment for processing and said, “No, wait. It’s not freaky; it’s more than a coincidence.” She gave a bit of a giggle, and my mind began to wonder what was next. I knew that something was in store for me and there was a definite reason for the encounter, but what?

She asked me a few questions about myself and what I did. I shared my story with her starting with my decision to leave the sheriff’s department. I told her I didn’t know what was in store for me, but I knew it was something far greater than I could imagine at the time. I was in a place where I didn’t know who I could talk to. I didn’t know what I was feeling at the time, but I did know something was missing.

I continued by telling her that I was looking to create a space for women to meet and share what they were feeling, and maybe together, we could figure it out. I also shared with her my desire to give a TED Talk. Her response was, “Oh really? I’ve done a TED Talk, and I can help you get there, and I do women’s retreats. It may be too close for you, but I have one coming up in November, and I would love for you to attend. Tell you what, how about I send you the info, and we go from there.” Now I had goosebumps all over, and my stomach was doing a happy dance.

Meeting Chauncey was a solid confirmation from a source unseen but felt. There was a sense of knowing all of what I was experiencing was in my destiny. The key was to be fully present in every moment of my day. For the first time did I really understand what was meant by, "There is a lesson in every experience." Now, the challenge that remained would be communicating that to my family, my husband.

November 2016 (Ready Woman) I Gotta Go, Babe

So, I found myself still buzzing because of the way the day had unfolded. There was a part of me that was excited to get home and share it with my family, but it hit me that it could result in a big blow-up instead.

After Doris dropped me off at the mall, I got into my truck, and I was on top of the world with joy and anticipation! I could hardly wait to share my day with my family. I was one of the first ones to return home, and one by one, the others came in. I immediately grabbed the laptop and googled her name, "Chauncey Beaty," and found her on YouTube.

I could feel a series of goosebumps beginning to flutter down my spine and then begin to slowly sunder throughout the remainder of my body as I shouted out loud with joy. I finished watching the TED Talk, went to the website she'd given me for the Ready Woman Retreat. I was so incredibly excited, and in awe, I wanted to cry again. Are you flipping kidding me?! GOD! YESSSSSS!! Once again, that someone or something I could not see or touch had shown up to give me what I asked for.

As I paced back and forth between the kitchen sink and the dining table, I tried to decide on the best angle to approach my husband. I was truly longing to share all of the magical events of the day with him, and then reality began to set in. I could feel it all completely spiral to the ground. I already knew he was going to think I had absolutely lost my mind, but I didn't care. I also knew within my entire being it was a clear "nudge" for me to go in that direction. The Universe presented to me a necessary road trip and made it perfectly clear without verbally saying or writing it on a wall: "GO, I GOT YOU."

So I took a few deep breaths while standing in front of my laptop sitting on the kitchen counter. I'd already begun to check fares on Southwest Airlines, and I had a car on reserve. Honestly, I'd already decided to go, but I still needed to take care of the technicalities of talking to my husband and children about what was happening.

I entered the bedroom where I found him lying down with his hands behind his head watching television. I hesitantly said hello and began to share my experience of the day. I told him that I met a really cool lady in the bathroom and she not only did wellness retreats, but she'd done a TED Talk. Unimpressed, he responded with a "Yeah and…?" I continued with, "She is having a retreat in November and has invited me to join them." "Yeah and where is this retreat?" he replied. I told him it would be in South Carolina from November 6th–9th.

He said, "And you want to go to South Carolina?" I responded with, "Umm, ye- yeah, I really do. I know it all seems pretty crazy, but I really, really think I'm supposed to be there. I wish I could tell you why, but I really don't know how to explain it to you right now."

My husband was so confused and frustrated with me that he didn't know what to say or how to respond to what appeared to him to be completely irrational thinking on my part. All I heard was him say, "Then go, Felicia, just go," and that was all I needed. Honestly, I didn't need it, but I was looking for him to help me see that there was nothing wrong with me. You see, even if my husband had said no, I would've followed what I was feeling anyway. There was something that was happening to me and I had to go in the direction I was being guided.

There was a part of me that was hoping to go with his blessings. Don't ask me why! Hell, I thought maybe he would wish for me to find what I was looking for so that our family could get back on track or at least close to how it used to be. Maybe my coming to him with this incredibly out of the ordinary request to do something that was so off my baseline would prompt him to be supportive maybe lay a kiss or hug on me. Ha-ha—not.

If I've learned nothing else, I've learned that when it comes to faith and belief in yourself, sometimes you just need to be willing to not give a shit about what your family or anyone else thinks or has to say about what you may be doing. No one—and I mean no one—will ever be able to tell you what is good for you. There is not another human being on this planet that knows what is best for you better than you do—period. I was feeling something deep, something that I had never felt before. I didn't just *want* to go to South Carolina, I *needed* to go. It was a part of the journey. What I was feeling was so strong that nothing and no one was going to get in the way of me getting there.

Planes, Trains and Automobiles

Frankly, I think it shocked Chauncey when I told her I was coming. Not that she didn't believe it, but I would imaginc that most people don't follow through on something that could be making a decision on a whim. I know I've never met anyone in the ladies room I didn't know before going in only to find myself deciding I would go to her event in SC nearly two weeks later.

I booked a flight on Southwest Airlines from Seattle to Chicago to Atlanta. I wasn't familiar with Hilton Head, South Carolina. In fact, I'd never even heard of it until after meeting Chauncey. The goal was to make the trip and spend as little money as I possibly could. After landing in Atlanta, I rented a car and began my next leg of the journey which was a four-hour solo drive to Hilton Head Island.

I can remember getting into the car and slowly making my way out to the airport terminal. It was almost as though I was gliding, like I knew the route and the exact way to go. There was no fear or hesitation; there was a knowing I was exactly where I was supposed to be and it felt incredibly delicious. I felt so alive! The journey was unbelievably breathtaking. As I drove, I couldn't help but take it all in completely, the smell of the pasture, cows, sheep and chickens. I loved the sounds of the cars and trucks as they made their way down the highway going east and west and

I wondered if any of them had ever felt what I was feeling? I couldn't be the only one that was feeling this way.

Then there it came again, "Breathe and know that it's all okay. You are exactly where you are supposed to be at this moment. Have no concern about the others; it is only you this moment is for right now. Drive my love and know that it will work out just as it should. You have asked for guidance and understanding; continue to listen and trust and you will."

The drive to Hilton Head didn't feel like it was even close to a four-hour drive. I stopped for gas once on the way for about half an hour from my destination. The homes were like the ones you've seen in movies and on TV, but the difference was you could feel the energy, and presence that was surrounding the properties as I passed by them, especially the ones that sat back from the main road surrounded by acres upon acres of land leading to the main house.

As I pulled into the driveway of the property, there was a feeling that overcame me, a feeling once again of being exactly where I was supposed to be. I struggled not to shout out loud, thinking that if someone heard me they would wonder what the hell was going on. So, I took a deep breath and reminded myself to relax and just be cool. I got out of the car and just stared for a moment at the incredibly beautiful home in front of me. It was three stories tall and it looked like something out of one of those fancy home magazines. I retrieved my bags from the back of the car and headed towards the stairs leading to the home. As my right foot touched the first step, I had an urge to run up the stairs so that I could match the beautiful voices to the faces of the women I would be spending the next three days with.

I am still completely fascinated to this day by the orchestration of the Universe and the way it brought together twelve women of various ages, walks of life and regions together. Each of us was longing and desperate to understand what we were experiencing. Our need to be understood by those whom we shared our lives with outside of the circle of women we didn't even know existed until then.

We each knew our gathering was not one of luck or chance. It was by divine design. It only took moments before we found ourselves completely enchanted with seeing ourselves in the other, knowing it was because each of us decided to go with our belief, no matter how it came to us of being in this space at this time, together. Here there was no concern about sharing what we were thinking, feeling and experiencing because of it.

Our paths did not cross by chance or happenstance. We were each guided by divine design. We opened our hearts and souls and poured out all the pain, wounds, scars, fears, and disappointments. We were kindred souls, each and every one of us, connected by an invisible thread. It would be the first time that I would have such an experience, but not the last. The pain of one was felt by all. It was time to clean house and only those who were ready and willing to let go and allow themselves to step fully into the unknown would receive all that the universe had in its beautiful treasure box. Looking at yourself in the mirror is deeper than the reflection. It is the willingness to stand in the truth of your journey, looking at who you thought you were versus who you are destined to be. It was the opening of a door for clarity that would take place in the others' pain as if it were our own, with no holds barred. There was nothing off limits. The part of us that spent the time together over those three days would remain with me forever, for as long as I live.

The TED Talk & Fairy Dust

March 2016

Several years ago, I stumbled upon a speech that was given via the TED Talk platform and I was hooked. I often found myself completely fascinated with the variety of topics and innovative ideas that were being shared around the world. I'd never been a huge movie fan or TV fanatic, but rather one who enjoyed hearing or viewing thought-provoking material that was outside the norm.

It was the early spring of 2016. I placed my laptop on the kitchen countertop, googled TED Talk and hit the automatic tap so they would play one after the other as I prepared a meal for my family. As I cut the onions and celery, I listened to one then another, and they were all awesome as always. As I cut the onions and celery, I glanced at the clock to check the time so I wouldn't be late picking up my son from school. I didn't want to be in the middle of the next task without finishing it.

I looked to see what the topic was and thought, "Who cares, just let it ride." I resumed cutting and dicing all while listening haphazardly to the speaker. Then I heard the words, "Fairy Dust" and I whipped my head around to face the laptop. I blew up the screen and I stared at the speaker.

I mumbled, "Fairy dust. Who is she?" I scrolled down the screen and I said, "Is that her? That's the lady that wrote the book!" What?! Is that Elizabeth Gilbert?" I began to laugh hysterically and jump around the kitchen, dancing and doing high kicks and jumping jacks! It was like I had discovered a new invention or won the Powerball lottery. I was so incredibly happy at that moment because I knew it would lead me to the next step of my amazing journey. She was talking about fairy dust! It was the same fairy dust she spoke about in her book, *Big Magic*! I love it! It's her!

I smiled to myself, glanced out my kitchen window as I looked over into the sun and thought to myself without ever saying a word, "It's going to be really cool to meet her." It was a brief thought and then—poof—it was back to cutting the onions and celery. I didn't think about it again.

Sister Road Trip / Damien E.

June 2016

Hey Music Man!

Just when I began to wonder what I would do next, that's when I heard the sound of a violin as I'd never heard it before. The way this guy played those strings sent chills up and down my spine and made my head feel as though it was about to explode with boundless joy! I shrugged my shoulders back and just stared at him as he played.

I felt as though I was there with him, connected to him, somehow, some way. It was as if this magical tune was created to produce something that had been waiting to be unlocked. I know it sounds crazy, but I felt as if there was a message in the sound of the strings on his violin, and that is when I began to write. It was like something that I could not see was communicating to me in a form that was different from anything I had experienced in my life. The music man had entered the picture, and I was living in Washington State. I was in the kitchen when I got the urge to call my sister, Debbie, and invited her to join me on a road trip that would once again take me to another level of being.

During the first week of June, I called my sister, Debbie, and I asked her if she would be up for a road trip. She laughed, called me a fool and then asked, "Where?" I said, "I don't know, anywhere. Maybe we could go down to Mississippi. I've never been there! Maybe we should see if the dirt is really red like Momma used to say. Do you think we can really eat it? Come on, let's just go!" We ended the call agreeing to make a decision on which direction we wanted to go.

I opened my laptop to begin my research on Mississippi and my Facebook page opened on the screen and there he was. Damien Escobar was playing that tune and it ignited me to begin writing. This time, instead of writing, I decided to Google his name and concert. No way! Turns out, he was on tour. I looked at the calendar and saw that he was going to be in Philly later in the month.

Without thinking, I checked out the theater for his concert seating availability, booked two tickets and called my sister back immediately. I asked her if she'd heard of this guy. She told me no, but I was so full of excitement that I felt like I wasn't making sense. I slowed down enough to explain to her that he was the violinist that ignited my writing. I asked her what she thought about going to the East Coast instead of heading south. “I’ve never been to D.C. before!” I explained to her. “What do you think?”

She agreed. Yes! Only after that did I tell her that I’d purchased two tickets to see Damien Escobar at the Neptune Theatre in Downtown Philly. I told her the dates, and that I would check on flights to Chicago. From there, we could begin the road trip after her last day of school.

After ending the call, I booked my flight on Southwest Airlines, secured a condo in downtown Philly, and reserved a rental car to pick up later on the twenty-third of June so that we would be on the road early in the morning on the twenty-fourth. Everything flowed without effort. It was like sheer magic.

We threw our bags in the car and hit the road, stopping in Columbus, Ohio after our first six hours to spend the night with one of our first cousins, Deanne. After catching up and sharing childhood memories over dinner, we headed home to get some rest. In the morning, we had a quick cup of coffee, thanked her for the hospitality and hit the road again. It was so invigorating! We felt like two free birds soaring through the sky! Living life and loving every moment of it.

During our travels, I found myself being drawn to strangers along the way. I began to tune in more to everything around me, and the more I opened my heart, the more it seemed as though complete strangers were drawn to me and vice versa. As I shared more of my thoughts with my sister, she too was beginning to see first-hand what I was talking about when it came to people being beautiful and they really just wanted someone to show they cared. Loving people is what I was doing. Sharing my life with them, if only for a brief moment, was spreading within my soul like a wildfire.

I would say hello to someone and ask them how their day was going and if they were doing okay. Sometimes I would ask them what their passion was and if they were enjoying life. Don't even ask me where I got the courage to do that, it just flowed naturally. What business was it of mine, right? But here's the thing, they were all very receptive, not one person I had crossed paths with was rude or standoffish. I eventually found it to be quite easy to do. And by simply doing that, I was telling complete strangers that it's okay for them to join me as well, by just being open.

It was exciting to be on the road with my sister, taking in the sights and sounds of life. We traveled through Ohio and passed through Virginia as we made our way to Washington D.C. to see the White House. While in D.C., we found ourselves in awe of many of the monuments: the Martin Luther King Jr., Lincoln Monument, the Korean War Veterans Memorial (of which our father served). The National World War II Memorial is breathtaking, especially if you see the fountain at night.

I had a dear friend put a challenge on social media to do 22 pushups for 22 days as a way to bring awareness to the increasingly alarming rate of suicide among veterans. There we were, standing in the middle of it all when I remembered I hadn't completed my pushups that morning.

So what did I do? You got it, I hit the ground. People were walking all around looking, wondering even taking some pictures. My thoughts were, this is not by chance or happenstance. It made me even more excited to have taken the challenge that Ski threw at me.

I rose daily with a sense of gratitude for it all and even more for my husband and children being open to my going on this trip. After all, it was summer and they were out of school for the year. One may ask why they didn't go with us. There are reasons for everything that happens and sometimes we don't know what they are until later. At the time, I felt the pull to go east with a final stop in Philly for the concert and then head back home.

We decided to stop for lunch outside of the Philadelphia area and my sister asked how much the condo cost. I told her, and in return, she stated that it was far too expensive and suggested that we find something cheaper. I told her I had it covered. Besides, the condo was very close to the venue, so we could walk and take in some of the city. My sister insisted that we look for something else. I was hesitant because the concert was sold out, we didn't know the area, we didn't know if anything else was going on, and most importantly, what if we couldn't find anything?

Reservation Cancellation

I canceled the Airbnb. We spent some time trying to locate a hotel or motel in the area where we could sleep for the night, only to be told time after time, "Sorry, we are sold out," or "Sorry, we have no rooms available at this time." We even had a woman at a Ramada Inn take our information and tell us she would give us a call as soon as she confirmed a reservation. She suggested that we could wait in the lobby, parking lot or grab some food.

We sat in the lobby for a bit, eventually making our way to the parking lot where we fell asleep in the car near one of the light posts. We were exhausted at that point and didn't care very much. We both began to laugh as we woke to the sounds of birds chirping near our car. Two middle aged women sleeping in the car on a road trip; we saved a lot of money that night, but that's the price you pay when you wake to have a catch in your hip and consciously take it slow as you raise the seat.

We were both shocked about what we had done and couldn't stop talking about what our mother would have thought and said if she knew. Even though our mother had been gone for many years, it was like we felt the same way we would've if she were still here.

Concerts, movies and celebrities never fascinated me growing up except for Foxy Brown, Coffee and Kristie Love who were my idol characters, but otherwise, they didn't do anything for me. So my desire to see this violinist in concert was way out of the box for me.

I don't quite remember when I told my sister what my thoughts were several months before finding his tour calendar and purchasing the tickets. In fact, I hadn't mentioned it to anyone and thought it would be best to just keep it to myself. The first time I'd heard or seen him play was on a Facebook post, and it gave me goosebumps and a knowing that I would see him play live.

Sometime during our trip, I opened up to my sister and told her that I believed I was not only going to hear Damien

Escobar play, but I believed I was supposed to talk to him about something.

Studio 73

During the next several months, I would again find myself feeling a bit lost, not because I didn't know there would be a "next step," but because I wasn't producing an income to contribute to my household. I knew I couldn't continue to spend money that I didn't have because my family was eventually going to feel the pinch and that would only cause more issues.

I could feel the desperation that was sweeping over me. It was like I was grasping for straws, trying different things others were offering me to be a part of to create an income, but they just weren't for me. I was not able to talk to my husband and share with him what I was thinking or feeling for fear of having the pain of shame and embarrassment wash over me with my children standing front and center to see.

One day while on Facebook, I saw a post that a former coworker had shared regarding his home studio. I decided to give him a call. Eventually, we met up and I shared with him some of my experiences along with when and why I left my career. It was awesome to find that Mike and I had a lot in common, and although he had a bit more understanding of the good book, I was increasingly gaining knowledge every single day.

Mike and I ended up spending some time together in his home recording studio after he informed me about a website I could go to and find voice-over gigs and it was pretty cool. In time, I would find myself being the voice on eight different audiobooks. I smile and I smile wide because it was in March 2014 that I declared myself a voice-over talent to Pamela, someone I had just met in a hotel gym in downtown Chicago nearly three years before.

I grew bored and it wasn't as much fun as I thought it would be. It didn't matter at that point. My question to you at this moment is: Do you think that was a coincidence, happenstance, or luck?

Let The Music Play

We got to the theatre and I was so excited, I felt like I was going to burst from sheer joy. The crowd slowly began to cntcr and my heart was dancing. My mind was bouncing all over the place in the eagerness of what would unfold next. I pinched myself a couple of times as I struggled with believing that what was happening was reality.

The theater was dark and a bit smoky. It reminded me of one of the theaters back home that were once the hot spots and the place to be if you were anybody worth knowing. It appeared to have been forgotten about over the years, and from the look of it, there hadn't been much funding going into restoring this historic building. Coming from Chicago and growing up with rats that would punk you in the alleys and threaten to take your popcorn at the Englewood Theater during the ninety-nine cent movie, I can't even begin to complain about this place.

Everything up to this point felt right, at least until we found our seats and I saw how far away they were from the stage. As we settled in, the lights began to dim with a little instrumental backdrop music to get the audience ready for the main attraction. I began to bob my head to the rhythm and sway my body in the seat, "Hey, that's what I'm talking about! Heeeeeyyy."

My sister looked over to me to see if the show was sold out. I told her it wasn't sold out, but there were very few tickets remaining. What I didn't realize was when I purchased our tickets we would find ourselves sitting in the nosebleed section of the venue. But hell, it didn't matter to me. I was about to witness an incredible artist play the several melodies of which my favorite "Awakenings" sparked something within me to begin writing.

As the concert began, I was completely locked on his every move. I could feel each string being played almost as if I was a part of everything that was happening. Moments before the intermission, the artist began to hand roses out to some of the women near the stage. Of course, I would've liked to have one of the roses, but I knew that wasn't going to happen. Thank goodness I had my big sister there to bump my arm to make sure I wouldn't make a mad dash through hundreds of people to get a rose.

So, I just sat there and took in the remainder of the concert and found myself feeling grateful for following that feeling, and although the rose didn't really matter much, I did wonder how our paths would cross and then I let go of the thought.

We listened to the closing number and he received a standing ovation! It was the best concert that I'd ever been to in my life! Okay, not that I've been to that many concerts. The crowd began to clear the theatre and as my sister and I entered the lobby, I still felt like it wasn't finished. My sister asked if I was disappointed and I said, "No, I just feel like, umm, I thought there was maybe something more." For some reason I believed I was going to speak with him. What was I going to say? Heck I had no idea. I was trying not to show my emotions as I began to feel like the embarrassed little sister. What if I was wrong about all of what I was "feeling"?

I looked over to see one of those big wall posters of him and told my sister to take a photo of me in front of it, and she did. I said, "Maybe I was supposed to talk to the poster?" Then I noticed several people standing in a line on the other side of a divider. I leaned over to one of the women and asked, "What's happening here? What's the line for?" She responded with, "If you want to take a picture with Damien, this is the line for it." I say to my sister, "Deb? I'm going to take a picture with him. What do you think?" She said, "Cool!" As I hopped in the line, the woman in front of me told me that I needed to pay to take a picture. I said, "Really? How much does it cost?" Her response was $25. My sister's eyes got quite large and you could clearly see she was disturbed by this.

I didn't have much cash on me, so I asked my sister to loan me the money to pay for the photo. She told me that I shouldn't pay to take a picture with him, but I made it clear to her that I really wanted one. She agreed and I continued to stand in the line awaiting my turn. I was trying to keep my sister cool about having to pay for the photo by making small talk.

Before I knew it, it was my turn. I walked over to where he was standing, and I began to pretend that I was in a boxing ring with him. Yeah, I know right? I didn't make contact; I was just pretending to punch him. I think that is just something that I do when I'm a bit nervous about something. Anyway, he laughed a little and reached his hand out to shake mine. When he did, he quickly pulled it back and shook it out as he said to me:

DE: “Whoa! You have some serious energy!”

Felicia: (Embarrassed) “Umm, yeah, I do. Sorry about that. You okay?”

DE: “Yeah I’m good. (Laughing) Do you get told that often?”

Felicia: “Umm, yeah, more lately than ever.”

DE: “Where are you from?”

Felicia: “I’m originally from Chicago, but I live in Seattle.”

DE: “Oh, okay. Seattle, huh?”

Felicia: “Yeah.”

DE: “So, I guess I need to put Seattle on my next tour?”

Felicia: “Yes, indeed you do. Anyway, I don’t want to take up too much of your time but, you really need to be careful of the circle that you are keeping. You’ve been given a second chance at this, so don’t mess it up. Got it?”

He looked at me and didn’t know what to say. I looked at him and said, “Take care of yourself okay? I gotta go now. It was nice to meet you. Bye.”

My sister and I could not stop laughing. My sister was shocked by what had just happened and how it all fell into place. I smiled and winked at my sister. Later, I would share with her that what happened was an example of what had been happening to me regularly since experiencing the four coincidences during my visit to Chicago when I was there for Patricia's funeral services.

She looked as though she had an "a-ha moment," like she couldn't believe it, but was willing to stay open to it. I was beyond grateful to have her by my side as a witness of that moment. Again, I wanted to cry but we opted to go get a Philly steak sandwich instead. Food always makes it better.

The following year, Damien Escobar came to Seattle and played at the Neptune Theatre where I again had the opportunity of seeing him in concert and it was incredible.

Blurred Vision On A.M. Radio

March 2017

It was one of those cold, wet and rainy days that you were sure to find if you lived in Washington State where it rains nearly ten months out of the year. I didn't like it when I first moved there, but I quickly realized that I could do one of two things: learn to be okay with it or spend year after year being upset about not having as much sunlight and falling into a state of depression repeatedly.

So as I stood at the front door looking out at the rain falling, I went through a series of emotions. From being angry to being excited, because I knew once I got to moving, it would all be okay. I eventually threw myself out in the rain and I was putting one foot in front of the other. I would soon find my rhythm and get into the groove of the music that was playing in my headphones. I was going uphill, breathing in the clean, crisp air of the morning and feeling the thrill of being alive!

I decide to run in the direction of one of the neighborhood coffee houses where I had reserved their meeting room several weeks before to facilitate my fitness and wellness workshop. As I entered the front door, there was a woman who simultaneously entered the door leading into the shop from the off-street parking lot. We made eye contact, smiled and said good morning.

The shop was flowing with customers and the owner was a bit tied up with orders, so I stood there for a bit. I found myself being drawn to this woman. The energy was so incredibly strong, I could not ignore it. I walked over to her and introduced myself.

Me: "Good morning."

Shelia: "Morning."

Me: "Are you here for the workshop?"

Shelia: (Excitedly) "Workshop? Oh, there's a workshop here today? What kind of a workshop?"

Me: "I'm facilitating a fitness and wellness workshop on the upper level in the conference room. I thought I'd stop by to see how many folks were signed up."

Shelia: "How exciting! But, uh no, I wasn't here for the workshop. I was here to meet one of the pastors of a church I attend."

I asked her what she did for a living and she shared that she was the creator of a program that helps others manage their weight from a psychological standpoint. She shared that she had undergone one of the surgeries to help her lose weight on her personal journey. Having majored in psychology, she was currently a candidate on the Ph.D. list.

I shared with her a bit of my weight loss journey and that I'd competed in several NPC Figure/Bodybuilding competitions, and as a result, came to realize it begins from the inside out and not vice-versa. I was super thrilled to have met her. We exchanged information and decided to meet at a later date for a cup of coffee or tea.

Sheila and I met for coffee soon after. Our conversations were so insightful and incredibly creative that hours would go by unnoticed. It felt as though we would know each other for years. Our friendship continued to grow as we shared our ideas, hopes and dreams. It felt almost too good to be true.

Then Sheila offered me to be a part of her company. She thought I would be great as the VP and was excited about my ability to grow the company from the ground up. Sheila liked the way I spoke to others and would often tell me that I had a gift of including everyone which would be great for business. I was a bit puzzled as to her willingness to split everything 50/50, but instead of pressing the pause button and thinking it through, I ignored it and continued on.

We met with several professionals, from a represent-tative of an afterschool program to an independent film director to a radio host. With each encounter, I began to take notice of the way she would introduce herself and the importance of letting others know she was on the Ph.D. candidate list. I decided to brush it off time and time again, thinking, "To each his own." Just because I didn't see titles as a priority doesn't mean that others had to agree with my thinking.

I wondered what would become of my brand and found myself straddling the fence on what to do, and my indecision left me feeling uneasy. Over some time, my voice became less heard and it wasn't dancing with the same excitement as before making her acquaintance. I attempted to push forward anyway and tried to see beyond the little things that would eventually become big things to me. The thought of telling my husband and children the collaboration was a flop paralyzed me with the fear of embarrassment and shame, so I kept my mouth shut and kept pushing forward. We managed to get through a couple of workshops that were a struggle for me. She appeared to have a need for complete control regarding the format and material covered; it was killing me inside. Yet I continued to press on.

Then I spoke of being on a radio station. I thought it would be a great opportunity to land a segment to be able to advertise the business. Score! We landed a noon spot at a local station once a week. I sent a notice out to my family and several friends of when to listen for the debut. There we were, live on the air. She even posted it to Facebook. I couldn't believe it! After the show, we decided to talk about how it went; pros and cons what we could've done differently and so on.

I walked away thinking, "What did I do right in the show?" There seemed to be an incredible amount of criticism on what I needed to correct. I left thinking I should embrace it and grow from it instead of feeling beat up on.

We met a few times during the week, and before our next show, to decide on a topic. We decided on mental health, which I thought was awesome. We broke it down into how and what area we would discuss before the show so we wouldn't run out of time to offer information to our listeners on where they could seek help, whether it was for them or someone they knew.

Showtime: We were on the air, and during the first segment, I couldn't seem to get a word in edgewise. You would've thought it was a one-woman show. I actually wondered if she practiced holding her breath at home because it seemed as if she was talking without ever taking in a breath. But then she did, and I added a comment to something that was said to lighten up the academic part of it. The plan was to educate and still stay on the lighter side of life, so I decided to throw something comical into the smart wave and got a look of "what the hell are you doing?" shot at me.

She picked it up again, and honestly, was losing me as a listener and I was sitting across from her. Again I threw in my two cents, and again, I got that look with a rolling of the eyes and a sigh as we completed the first segment of the broadcast and went into a commercial break.

> During the break, it was quite clear that she was extremely irritated and asked:
>
> Sheila: "What are you doin'?"
>
> Me: "I was trying to lighten it up a bit. (light laughter) It was becoming too academic, don't you think?"
>
> Sheila: "Will you not do that?"
>
> Me: "What? We really should keep it light, Sheila. People get turned off when they feel like they can't understand what's being said; they can't relate."

Sheila: “Please don’t do that, every time you interrupt, you make me lose my train of thought.”

Me: “You got it.”

On Air:

Sheila picked up right where she left off and you wouldn’t have known that I was still in the studio because there wasn’t another word that passed my lips.

After the show, we were outside the studio. Sheila asked, “What was that about?” I sighed and replied, “You know, I think I need to take a step back from this. I’ll call you in a few days or so. It’s not quite what I thought it would be compared to our conversations when we weren’t on the air. Anyway, have a good week. Talk to you later.”

As we began to walk to our cars, it was like an unspoken acknowledgment between the two of us that our season together was complete. The inner guide within me rang the bell and sent me on my way with a smile and a sense of knowing that I’d received the lesson intended. Clearly, it was always to remain true to who you are no matter what. It took a while to make the connection of how I was feeling to whether I was going in the right direction, and that was okay. I still had some learning to do and I was getting better at recognizing the signs, clues and nudges from the Universe. I just needed to remember not to panic.

Answers In The Desert

After leaving the radio station, I headed straight home. I put my handbag on the sofa grabbed my MacBook and sat at the dining table. I opened the browser to Southwest Airlines and immediately booked a flight to Las Vegas. Was this going to cause a fight? I didn't know and frankly and didn't care. What I did know was it was imperative that I go south, and I needed to go south and fast.

I was on auto-pilot. My mind was made up about going to Las Vegas and there was no room for discussion. I didn't ask my husband if he would mind if I went out of town. I needed to go and nothing else mattered. When I saw my husband, I shared with him my plan to visit our home in Nevada for about a week or so. I tried my best to explain to him that I was a bit confused and I needed some space to think things over and find out which direction I needed to go. Was he okay with it? Absolutely not. He was as irritated as ever and shot back at me, "I just don't understand you, Felicia. I mean, put yourself in my shoes for a minute. Have you even thought about how you would react if I did even a quarter of the things that you've been doing? I mean, seriously, do you think you would be okay with this if you were me?" He gave me a smug look, shook his head and walked away.

Well, I had no way of truly knowing how I would feel if I were in his shoes, but I wanted to ask him the same question. How would he feel to have his life change so drastically? It sometimes felt unreal, to have the urge to go somewhere based on a feeling, and when you get there you know it was all happening precisely the way it should've. It was like a living scavenger hunt, except all of the clues were within you. It was a loving challenge to rediscover what your time here was really about, it's the purpose.

After landing in Las Vegas, I hopped in an Uber and headed for the house. Over nearly three days, I found myself planted in the middle of the sofa, just sitting. I didn't even turn the lights on; I just sat. The only time I would get up was to go to the bathroom and get a glass of water. It was strange, but cool. It was peaceful, quiet, still.

As the third day rolled around, I felt the urge to open my laptop. I went to the Groupon site, I typed in yoga. Then I changed it to hot yoga. There were like five thousand hot yoga facilities in and around Henderson and Las Vegas. Thirty days for $30 bucks. Yep I want one. Oh boy, what a deal. I registered and I got set for the morning class.

Morning came, and I was pumped and eager to get to class. It was quite the wake-up call when you remember how out of shape you are when it comes to different forms of exercise. That class kicked my ass. I thought I was going to die! No, wait, I meant that seriously. But somehow, I made it through and I was determined to get better, so I began going twice daily. During one of my visits, I noticed a business card that advertised meditation. My brother had suggested for some time that I try to include it in my daily routine. I started to pick up a card and declined.

A couple of days later, I checked out the yoga website looking for more information on the meditation class. I registered and put it on my calendar for the following Monday. During one of my visits to the last class of the evening, I saw a fellow working the front desk who looked an awful lot like the guy on the card. It was him. I stopped and we engaged in conversation, exchanging the basic pleasantries. Without hesitation, I began to share with him how I left my career after over twenty years and tried as best I could to explain to him what I was feeling. I went on to describe some of the strain it had placed on my marriage and the uncertainty it was creating for my children. Even with all of that, I had absolutely no regrets.

He replied with, "Sounds like you could use a little bit of 'the Work.'" I asked him, puzzled, "Who is that or what is it?" He turned and looked at me surprised and said, "You've gotta be kidding me? You don't know about the Work? Do you know who Byron Katie is?" I looked at him and said, "Ugh, no, please tell me more about it."

He asked if I had access to a computer. I said, "Yes, I have a laptop at home. What do I look for?" He suggested that I go online and google Byron Katie, School of the Work. I thanked him for the class and the information, wished him a good night and returned home.

As soon as I entered the house, I went directly for my laptop. I googled the name just as he'd suggested and up popped a gorgeous photo of a woman who had the warmest and most sincere eyes, and I could feel myself being drawn into the screen.

That feeling was upon me once again. It was a knowing of being on the right path. I felt immediately that I belonged there but I didn't know how that was going to happen, especially after I saw the cost. But even then, I didn't stop looking. I would open and close my laptop countless times just to look at the photo of the school or listen to the video clip that was on the site.

Desperation was seeping in, and I began to feel a sense of panic. I struggled to think of ways I could afford to go to the workshop. I wasn't working and yes, I had a credit card, but there was no way I was going to put myself in that position without a way to pay it off. Besides, if I did, my husband would completely blow his top and maybe even file for divorce on the basis that he believed I'd completely lost my mind and he didn't want anything more to do with it.

Eventually, I decided to let go and reminded myself that nothing should be forced and there was no need to stress out about anything. So, I decided to get back to being present, clearing my mind and enjoying my remaining yoga classes.

I hadn't visited the site for several days and then one night, I opened my laptop to find the website open already and a photo of Byron Katie. I smiled to myself and decided to scroll through again. Only this time I held the idea of requesting a payment plan. If I could do a payment plan than I could attend the workshop. In my mind, there was one idea that was shining bright and that was the light bulb of possibilities. After reading the information I decided, what the heck do I have to lose? If they say no, then so be it, but I wouldn't know unless I tried. I sat down and began to write; tears flowed down my cheeks, sharing with whomever would read my journey. I hit the send button and decided that I would not go back to the website again until I heard back from them. I began to focus my attention once again on where I was and what I was going to do when I returned home. Surely my husband was expecting that I would come up with a solution on how I would earn an income but I had none. For now, I was simply being, and feeling my way. I hadn't set any specific goals or deadlines and I trusted the next step would come to me.

August 2017:

Yes, yes, yes!!! They received my application request and it will be reviewed before the board!!! I felt like I'd won the lottery! The joy I felt within was about more than the possibility of attending the workshop. It was about me trusting that feeling and going for it without all of the panic!

Even if my application was a no-go after it was reviewed, I would be okay with it. I followed what I was feeling which brought me a tremendous amount of joy in and of itself, and now all I could do was wait on the final outcome of their decision. The request for clarity and understanding was out there and I knew somehow, sooner or later, it would come to me.

The Island Part Two

Fall 2017

After returning home from Nevada, I still couldn't tell you what lay ahead for me which was often unsettling. My life often felt as though it was beginning to spin out of control. I found myself thinking about what was happening to my marriage and desperately wanted to explain my thoughts and actions to my husband and children in a way they could understand, but I just didn't know how.

What I did know was it was one of the loneliest places to be and I was struggling within. I was trying to make sense of what had happened to me. I definitely knew I was not the same person I once was and I mean that literally, not just as a figure of speech.

Often I would cry myself to sleep on the sofa with Jaeger (my four-legged best friend ever). I could hear my children as they shared the stories of their day with my husband. Stories they once couldn't wait to share with us both, but now I felt excluded from. As the laughter rippled from our master bedroom and down the main hall, I found myself envious of him.

Was I being punished for being different, changing, following what I believed were messages from a source I could not describe or give a label to identify it? I wanted to scream loudly. The feeling of rejection by one's own family was excruciating. I wanted to believe it was unfair and even cruel, but I knew there had to be a reason behind why it was happening to me.

My heart felt like it sank deeper each time I tried to reach out to any of them. I really wanted them to at least try to understand what was happening to me. After all, I was just as confused as they were.

Nearly three years later, I would come to see "the island" wasn't such a bad place to be. There, is where I would find the space that was necessary for me to reconnect to my authentic self and my attachment to Source, God. I would realize in time that I'd detached from all of what I was connected through and my purpose for being here.

I looked the same, I sounded the same, I lived in the same house, I drove the same car, I had the same friends but—within—I was becoming someone they did not know. I was finally allowing me to meet me, and in time, I would truly understand I was already doing what I needed for them to understand.

October 2017:

I was still feeling a bit adrift and uncertain about what would be next. The atmosphere in my home at this point was so incredibly unwelcoming. My children were so angry with me for quitting my job, and from what they could see, I wasn't putting forth the effort to find another that could help take some of the pressure and financial burden off of their father. Often, I was even told I was at fault for his thinning hair. Ain't that a bitch? I found myself in a battle even with my children.

Generally, I could find a way to think about something that I was grateful for and it would turn things around for me emotionally. I never liked being stuck in that "woe is me" state, but sometimes it was tough to hold my chin up.

This particular day I can remember my heart feeling heavy and the onset of despair just around the bend. I'd once again had my feelings hurt because I was told that I was dreaming, it was an illusion and I was being brainwashed. If I thought something was going to drop out of the air and make everything alright, I was kidding myself. Fear was something that was ugly and powerful in my home, and at times discouraging, but I refused to be defeated by it.

I can remember one day thinking that I'm not going to get pulled into a fight and instead, decided to walk away. I went to our bedroom, locked the door, stood near the window and looked out at the trees on the trail and thought how beautiful it was to be a part of it all. I smiled at the people walking their dogs and wondered if they were happy. I began to cry and mumble to myself, "What am I going to do?" repeatedly.

At that moment, an email notification showed on the screen of my cell phone, and as I wiped my eyes to read it disappeared, but not before I saw the word "Work." I unlocked my phone and went to my email and there was a notification from the School of the Work with some additional questions for me.

I would eventually be given the green light to attend the school and it was one of the most exciting moments of my life. I felt like there was no one I could share it with who could relate. I did share it with my family, but no one was interested in hearing about another one of my wild adventures.

My husband was so angry that he gave me the silent treatment for several days. So I stopped sharing and decided to retreat to the island again. Sure, it was lonely, but at least I had Jaeger and he loved me unconditionally.

Flight booked, packed and ready to go. My husband went out the night before with several other friends and came home completely tanked. I guess I couldn't blame him, in a way. He had no control over what was happening with his wife and he was afraid, but it's not like he would ever admit that to his family. He was a great provider and would do what he needed to do to make sure his family was taken care of, even if he believed his wife had lost her mind and could end up at one of the mental hospitals.

I didn't want to argue about anything, so I tried to make it a point to get into bed before he returned home. I had an early flight with a 5:30 a.m. check-in. The next time I opened my eyes, I glanced at the clock which read 5:12 a.m. I leaped ten feet out of bed, filled with sheer panic, sick to my stomach and a little light-headed. My eyes began to fill with tears and all I could think was, "I'm going to miss my flight and the shuttle to the property. Will they still allow me to attend if I'm late?"

My eldest daughter came up the stairs concerned, wondering what was going on. I had trouble speaking to her right away due to the lump in my throat. Finally out comes, “I’m going to miss my flight to L.A. and I don’t know what to do. Your dad can’t take me. He’s been drinking and I don’t think he would be sober enough to drive me.”

Out of my daughter’s mouth came the sweetest sound that I’d heard in a very, very, very long time: “It’s okay Momma. I can take you to the airport. I don’t mind. I can take you, Momma. Just let me go put my shoes on and we can go, okay?” Then came that voice within that reminded me: “Breathe. Now call the airlines and let them know that you need to reschedule your flight.” The reservation agent had the voice of an angel. She adjusted the flight and informed me that I would receive a $7 refund on the next outbound flight to L.A.

I get to L.A. only not to understand where I was to catch the shuttle if I’d missed the first one. I reminded myself to breathe and not panic, but I also knew that in the instructions, it was clear that the shuttle would leave without me. Not wanting to arrive at the location late, I asked one of the shuttle services outside of the airport the cost of transportation to the property and thanked them. Then I stepped back to scratch my head and ponder what to do.

I tried reading the information again, thinking maybe that I missed something in the information packet. Out of fear of missing anything, I went back and reserved a space with the shuttle representative and paid nearly $200 which was more than the flight from Seattle to L.A. roundtrip and the original shuttle combined, but I didn’t care. At that point, it didn't even matter. I had somewhere to be and I was going to get there no matter what.

Shortly after getting into the van, I noticed that I was the only passenger, which was cool, just in case I went into another one of my sobbings. The driver received a call on the radio, turned to apologize for the delay, and explained that he had to make a stop to pick up another passenger. I said, "No worries." She boarded the van and there was a light about her that was so refreshing. She had skin the color of a cocoa bean and the sparkle of a midnight sky, full of stars in her eyes. She was Shanine, one of the coolest women I'd ever met who would drop a blunt in the middle of a crowd, pick it up, and offer it with love to the person standing next to her. I was elated to find that Shanine and I were headed to the same workshop.

We arrived on the property, and I was blown away! All I could do was think about myself as being that little chocolate chip from the south side of Chicago, and here I was standing in a place that people only dreamt of. It seemed too real to be true, but it was. I checked in and took a golf cart taxi to my room.

As I walked in, I noticed the person I would be sharing the room with was present. I felt such an overwhelming sense of love for this lady and I didn't even know her name.

Susan was yet another angel that was sent my way. She asked if I were okay with her having the bed closest to the window. Speaking with a bit of a southern accent, she said, "Now if you hear me snoring, please let me know right away because my husband says that I snore sometimes."

She was such a gentle, kind soul. Up to that point, I don't think I'd met anyone like her.

Susan was hearing impaired and I would've never known had she not apologized for the times I was talking and she missed what I was saying. I was so excited about everything that was happening at the workshop and could hardly wait to get back to our room so we could share our day. Sometimes Susan would have to remind me to slow down when she had to read my lips or give her a moment to change the battery.

She and I had an awful lot in common as well, but the one thing that I really loved about Susan was the man she'd married, Gary. I had yet to meet him, but he too from what she'd shared was a kind and caring soul, one that in time I knew I would have the pleasure of meeting. In any case, I was the luckiest person at the workshop to have scored the best roommate ever!

The Look A Like

It was our second day into the workshop and we'd just broke for lunch. Susan and I were like two giddy school girls skipping, rocking our heads as we walked towards the dining hall with our arms interlocked. Susan placed her right hand on my right hand.

Susan: "Did you see who's in our class?"

Felicia: "Who's in our class? You, me and a whole bunch of other folks who are here to get some understanding for themselves."

Susan: "No silly. I think it's Liz."

Felicia: "Liz? Okay, Good for Liz."

Susan: "I think it's Liz Gilbert."

Felicia: (Suddenly stops) "Susan? Are you kidding me?"

Susan: "Well now, don't hold me to it, but she looks an awful lot like her. Besides, she's been sitting behind you for the last two days."

Felicia: (Very laid back) "Susan, if it is her, remind me to share something with you when we get back to our room tonight."

Susan and I entered the dining area to have our lunch and were returning to the main study hall. Susan remembered there was something that she wanted to retrieve from the room before the next session started. I told her I'd head back to check our seats and make sure we still had pillows. She gave me a thumbs up.

There was a feeling of true appreciation of where I was and all of the beautiful people that I was surrounded by as I walked back to the main hall. I stopped in the lobby for a glass of water. As I entered the hall, I could see her sitting with her floor seat turned towards the opposite wall and she was writing in her journal. She was seated just behind me as Susan had explained. Without thinking about how big of a deal this was, I walked over and knelt on the floor next to her and began:

> Felicia: "Excuse me? I'm sorry to interrupt your writing but… (pause)… No, no I'm not sorry to interrupt your writing. I just wanted to say thank you for your creation of *Big Magic*. I believe your book kept me off of medication. Thank you so much for writing it."

She placed her journal and pen on the floor to the right of her, smiled and replied something to the effect of, "You are so very welcome," as she placed both her hands over her heart and then together. She gave me a hug and began to kiss my face over and over again. She extended her arms and then pulled me in for another hug and began doing the kissing thing again. It was clear that she was happy to hear me say it. I opened one of my eyes and said, "Umm, you can let me go now and go back to your writing. That was all I wanted to say. Thank you so much."

She gave a little chuckle, blew me a kiss with both hands as I nodded my head, smiled and returned to my floor seat. Susan's seat was positioned to the left of me with a pillow and blanket awaiting her return. As I settled into my seat, I found myself smiling, thinking my interaction with Liz was pretty cool. Shortly after, a sheet of paper came flowing across my shoulder with the words, "Thank You" written inside the drawing of a heart. I again smiled and nodded my head without looking back at her and knew something truly incredible had just happened. It was yet another "God wink" moment.

The other participants began to slowly return to the hall for the start of the next session. From that moment nearly every morning, she would greet me with open arms and several kisses. We would hold hands and smile. It was such a beautiful feeling. But here's the really cool part. I was feeling that way about everyone who was there. They were all beautiful people. I couldn't remember giving and receiving so many hugs and kisses in my entire life and it was great!

As the workshop came to a close, it was suggested that the participants exchange information so that we could continue to use what we had learned to allow us to live a more joyful and fulfilling life. The hall was full of love, laughter, life and a sense of hope that we could now find some understanding to some of the issues we had previously. I could hear someone from across the hall calling out my name, but I was not sure who was calling me. I heard it again. I looked up to see the biggest smile. It was Liz shouting that she wanted to work with me.

Now again, I will ask, do you think our encounter was a coincidence, happenstance or luck? The first time that I can even recall reading or seeing anything remotely attached to this person was in February 2014. There was a Facebook post that came across my feed with Glinda the good witch from the Wizard of Oz. I didn't really know who she was other than there was a book titled, *Eat, Pray Love* then a movie about the book starring Julia Roberts, but that was all.

Over the years, I began to see the book in various places, bookstores, coffee houses and even garage sales which is where I would buy my copy, only to store it amongst so many other books I had the intention of reading eventually. I would even pick it up from time to time, touch the cover and put it back in the box. I can't help but laugh about it because it is hilarious. Only at this moment I realize that it had been summoning me for years and our paths were destined to cross.

How about you? Is there something that has been calling out to you? It often doesn't appear with a flashing light on top. Some messages come to us continuously by way of coincidences, gut feelings, dreams, predictions and countless other ways.

There are several names and titles I've come to hear over the past several years like a mid-life crisis, life shift, awakening etc. There has been a lot on the line for me to include running the risk of losing relationships, family, friends, and associates as a result of my decision to go with what I was "feeling."

All I can tell you for now is, what I've come to know as my Inner Guidance/Spirit was calling on me to show up, to recognize, be receptive and willing to let go and trust what I was feeling. I had to trust these "nudges" no matter how crazy or completely out of my mind others may have thought I was, including me.

There's so much that we have been missing in our lives due to our detachment from an entity that we all are connected to, regardless of the label we attach to it. Maybe we should try pressing the pause button every now and again, slow down or even stop for a bit to take in the present moment and the realization that we are all a part of the whole.

So the next time you get that feeling, yeah the one that you can't quite understand or find challenging to describe. Pay attention to it. You may even be willing to go with it to see where it leads or maybe you won't. In either case, know that there is nothing wrong with you. You are an incredible gift to this Universe and there is no other that comes close to you. The moment we decide to stand in who we are is the moment our light shines so bright that others begin to see their own by making a connection to how we feel. So the next time you feel some funny kind of way and you don't quite get it, press the pause button and ask yourself, "What am I feeling and why?" Don't ignore it because you could be ignoring the opportunity to meet your true self, the one that came into the world to change the game.

I'm so thankful for having the courage to let go and trust that small, still voice within, that feeling of knowing there was something more. Sure, it still gets dark every now and again, but the difference is, I know it only happens when I am not being true to myself.

My husband has yet to truly understand what happened to his wife, we're still married taking each day as it comes. My children are who they are and one out of the three has begun to experience her own nudges. I will continue to press on and move forward as the journey does not appear to be complete and I don't know when or if it will ever be. What I do know is the feeling of being alive and connected to everyone and everything beyond what I ever could've imagined is continuously evolving. Now that I have experienced some of what awaits me on the other side, "letting go" to return to what was would be like a slow painful death to my soul.

So, buckle up and let's go for a ride on the roller coaster of life, babe.

With Love,

Felicia

Acknowledgments

Thank You, Universe for granting me all that I have asked for and more. To all the incredible teachers that appeared in any and every form, no words can express my humble gratitude for your guidance and encouragement along the way. Debra Pryor, Dennis Pryor, Janice Vicente', Dayna Hersey and Alyse Russell, thank you for your kindness, gracious patience and standing by my side from the very beginning. I am forever grateful to you for keeping me grounded, listening to my cries, heartache and frustration, but most of all, laughing, loving me unconditionally and trusting that I would weather the storm on this journey.

Vera Stephanie, I send you lots of love and appreciation for being my SheRo and creating waves before I even knew what they were. Debra Ann, I thank you for being the ever-present force of encouragement, the reminder for me to keep trying and to never give up. Dennis Lydell, I'll never forget the day I could understand and speak your language. You are truly one of my greatest teachers and I love you, brother. I am honored to walk by your side, and it brings me great joy to know you will no longer walk alone. Thank you to all the officer's past and present for your work at the Pierce County Jail/Sheriff's Department

Kari Sprotberry, David (Dr. Buff) Patterson, your presence has been monumental during the chapters of my life. Elizabeth Gilbert, Damien Escobar, Doris Hughes-

Green, Chauncey Beaty, Susan Hutchison Saunders, Byron Katie, Liz Dawn Donahue, and Sharon Blake, thank you so much for your opening your hearts and sharing countless words of encouragement. Hugs and kisses to all the incredible beings that I've had the pleasure of meeting and crossing paths with while on this journey.

I wish to express my appreciation to As You Wish Publishing. My editor/publisher Todd and Kyra Schaefer for their amazing support, enthusiasm and valuable guidance through this project. Thank you for creating an avenue for so many who will now share their journey by becoming a voice to be heard.

The reader:

Even if we have yet to meet, I am honored that you chose this book, it is not by chance, luck or happenstance; it is by design. You are holding this book because it was written as a gift from me to you. Now, maybe you will read it right away, give it to someone or carry it around for a while and that's okay too. It'll be here for you, waiting until you are ready for it. My hope is when you do begin to read it, you will discover the joy of being the gift that you've always been.

Remember, the smallest things often go unnoticed, yet create the greatest change. My life will never be the same as I once knew it to be. Yes, there are still bumps in the road when it comes to my family. The good thing is I know when the turbulence comes there is something incredible that is about to happen, I just need to get through the storm that won't last forever.

You see I am willing to go against the grain of what I've been taught and shown based on how I feel because I know it will lead me to crossing paths with someone who is waiting for me to show up to remind them of just how incredible they are. Yes, it has been a pretty wild ride for everyone, and it is only the beginning! Are you ready?

Some of the names have been changed to protect the privacy of others throughout my writing.

Thank you for sharing some of your life with me whether you read the entire book, a few pages or simply glanced at the title, it doesn't matter. I know you didn't pick this book up by chance or accident and you are right where you are supposed to be. Thank you for showing up!

~Felicia

About The Author

Felicia Shaviri is on a mission to tell everyone within earshot or afar the importance of the role they play in the world. A former Correctional Deputy turned author and Wellness Coach; Felicia believes every person can turn their life around regardless of the circumstances. "I stand fast with an unbending belief that there is always an opportunity to learn and grow with every experience. Each experience offers us endless possibilities to live the life we desire."

Felicia a native of Chicago's Englewood District, lives between Milton, WA and Henderson, NV where she resides with her husband and three children. Felicia is a Professional Fitness/Wellness Coach, Certified Life Coach, Voice-Over Talent and the Founder of SheRox Fitness and Wellness based out of Henderson, NV. www.sheroxfitness.com

Felicia has an incredible ability to connect with troubled teens and women. She has helped countless clients through her one on one, group coaching and wellness retreats.

You Are a Gift,

Felicia Shaviri

Made in the USA
Lexington, KY
28 June 2019